W9-BYI-672

Preaching
the Gospel
Anew

Saint Clement
Maria Hofbauer

Preaching the Gospel Anew

Saint Clement Maria Hofbauer

JOSEF HEINZMANN, C.SS.R.

TRANSLATED BY
BERNARD J. MCGRADE, M.A.

Liguori
LIGUORI, MISSOURI

Published by Liguori Publications
Liguori, Missouri

The original title, *Das Evangelium neu ver Künden: Klemens Maria Hofbauer,* was published by Kanisius Verlag, Freiburg/Schweiz.

Library of Congress Cataloging-in-Publication Data

Heinzmann, Josef.
    [Klemens Maria Hofbauer. English]
    Preaching the Gospel anew : Saint Clement Maria Hofbauer / Josef
Heinzmann : translated by Bernard J. McGrade.
        p. cm.
    Includes bibliographical references.
    ISBN 0-7648-0164-3
    1. Hofbauer, Klemens Maria, Saint, 1751–1820. 2. Christian saints—
Austria—Biography. 3. Redemptorists—Austria—Biography. I. Title.
BX4700.H55H4513 1998
282'092—dc21
[b]   97–53212

Copyright 1998 by Josef Heinzmann
English translation copyright 1998 by North American Chapter of the
Institute of Redemptorist Historical Studies (NA/IRHS)

02 01 00 99 98   5 4 3 2 1
First U.S. Edition

Contents

Editor's Preface

In spite of Napoleonic spies, French and Austrian anticlerical persecution, heartbreaking tragedies, and his own death before he could see any results, Clement Hofbauer's faith, his teachings, his friends, his students, and his Redemptorist Congregation survived to transform the post-Revolutionary period of the nineteenth century.

Saint Clement Hofbauer illustrates the challenges that may face anyone searching for holiness during a time as revolutionary as today. He helped spread forms of piety and preaching that were then revolutionizing Italian religious life to all of Europe. He was also at the center of the Restoration and Romantic movements in the Austro-Hungarian Empire and was named patron saint of Vienna.

The present translation of the popular German-language biography by Josef Heinzmann was sponsored by the North American Chapter of the Institute of Redemptorist Historical Studies (IRHS/NA). In conjunction with Liguori Publications, we are happy to make this book and the life of Saint Clement Hofbauer available to the English-speaking world.

We hope you enjoy the book.

PAUL LAVERDURE

Preface

A box on the ear—a box on the ear from a saint no less—
moved me to write this book. That may sound strange.
And yet it's quite true.

At the time I was in the novitiate. My decision was firm: I
wanted to become a Redemptorist. One day I was overcome with
awful doubts about my calling. "Should I really choose this path?
Will I make it? Or must I...." I tried desperately to find my way
out of the jungle of my questions and problems. But I became
even more tied up in the knots of *ifs* and *buts*. My spirit grew
darker and darker.

The next day, I plucked up my courage and admitted my confusion to my novice master. The good man had several solutions.
He pointed to the saints of the Redemptorist Order—they, too,
had to struggle and strive. Finally, he gave me a pile of books and
sent me back to my room.

Tired, I reached for the biography of Gerard Majella. It is
said of him that he worked miracles and that even as a boy he
fasted strictly. "And me? Oh, just the thought of the next fast day
makes me hungry." Then I took a book by our founder Alphonsus
Liguori. I read his small pamphlet *The True Redemptorist*. But—
oh misery! What a true Redemptorist must do and renounce.
"No!—Pointless! I will never make it!" I was already toying with
the idea of hanging up my habit and abandoning the novitiate.

But then something amazing happened. I was lazily browsing through a yellowed old volume on Saint Clement Maria Hofbauer. And—I did not believe my eyes. There, in black and white, it stated that as a mature man Clement had to struggle with his anger. One day this anger even came to an unseemly explosion. He boxed another member of his community on the ear and ran away. "What? How?" And he became a saint? "Let's go, Joseph," I said to myself "you can do it, too!"

He (the saint or his anger?) had worked a small miracle. My doubts about my calling disappeared. Since then, I like saints who are made of flesh and blood as we are. I even like the tortured, hot-blooded saints.

Clement Hofbauer is not a saint built on clichés. He was and remains a human being, by nature so impulsive "that he sometimes acted rashly and spoke harshly." He knew his weaknesses and did not excuse them. With a measure of self-irony, he admitted, "Yes, that is unfortunately my failing. And I thank God for it. It has kept me humble and saved me from pride. Had I not had this failing, I would be tempted to kiss my own hand out of respect for myself."

Into this somewhat rough vessel God placed a large heart. The meek and the poor, the abandoned and the failed found a selfless friend in him. Even the embarrassingly stubborn poet Zacharias Werner, who had once attacked our saint with a rare impertinence, praised him later as a good man: "Clement, you gentle man."

Clement Hofbauer does not fit any mold. One can barely explain his complicated life and rich accomplishments without occasionally stopping for lack of the right words. Clement was a hermit and a wandering apostle, a successful mixture of deep interior contemplation and active duty. As a hermit, he did not fall into a strange eccentricity, and as a missionary he did not give in to hectic activism. This man of faith was born into terrible times, into an anticlerical and antireligious century.

He had the courage to stand tall upon the ruins of his life's work and to believe in the mercy of God. As a missionary with a rare feeling for the sufferings of his time, he adapted his ministerial work to the concrete circumstances he faced. He tenaciously started a program of Christian renewal that amazes us to this day. Although his plans were regularly interrupted, he succeeded in creating a Catholic Reform Movement, which marked an entire era in German-speaking countries.

Wherever he arrived, he was a living symbol of contradiction. During his lifetime, many people admired and loved him because "this man inspires uncommon faith." On the other hand, he was attacked in the streets by his opponents. Official spies of various governments watched him closely. To them, he was a dangerously "talented and extremely cunning man." His name was always on the blacklist. At the end of his life, he said with a smile: "Many people have thrown themselves to the ground and kissed my footprints; three times as many have thrown mud at me. If some have dishonored me too much, others have honored me too much."

Writing the life of a saint is always a daring undertaking and must necessarily remain an attempt. The biography of Hofbauer is especially difficult to write because we know so little of the first thirty-five years of his life. In addition, Clement was forced by circumstances to destroy documents that would have been important to us. Once burned, twice shy. The police at the time knew that "Hofbauer destroys all letters." Even his personal correspondence with his family is lost.

Existing documents were collected and published in the fifteen volumes of the *Monumenta Hofbaueriana* in 1951. Scholars have recently succeeded in finding some new material. Also, various studies concerning Saint Clement Maria Hofbauer have appeared in the journal *Spicilegium Historicum Congregationis SSmi Redemptoris*. I have used these sources for this book.[1]

This biography intends to be popular but historically accurate. Daring to shed some light upon the personality and the ministerial work of our saint, I often quote him, his friends, and his opponents. Hofbauer's pithy statements reveal the inner essence of the saint better than any descriptions. After his trouble-filled life, he did indeed leave our world. Yet the saint is still among us: he has a message to give us.

I owe special thanks to my confreres, Fathers Anton Bazielich, Marian Brudzisz, Fabricano Ferrero, Alois Kraxner, and Hans Schermann. Each of them has been helpful in his own way. Above all, I owe the existence of this book to Father Provincial Hans Schermann. He inspired this biography and strongly supported it.

Part One

Clement Zigzags Toward His Goal 1751–1785

CHAPTER 1

Importance of Roots
1751–1767

Tasswitz lies about one hundred kilometers (sixty-two miles) north of Vienna. This southern Moravian farming village is in the Czech Republic. A young Slav named Peter Paul Dvořak turned up there around 1730. We do not know why this butcher's apprentice left his village of Budwitz.

In Tasswitz he met Maria Steer, the daughter of the village judge and butcher. Since his wife-to-be and the other villagers spoke German, Paul had his name changed to the German equivalent, Hofbauer or Hoffbauer, before the wedding. Paul and Maria were married on January 31, 1736, when the groom was twenty-four and the bride twenty. Since the young bride had been fatherless for quite a while, she brought her father's inheritance into the marriage: a house, a butcher shop, and a small farm.

The new family grew quickly, as the baptismal records of Tasswitz show. With regularity, one child was born after the other in the Hofbauer-Steer family: Anna Maria (1737), Karl (1738), Franz (1740), Maria Theresia (1742), Maria Barbara (1743), Hermann (1745), Lorenz (1747), Rosina (1750), Johannes (1751), Katharina (1754), Paul (1755); and the mother, Maria Hofbauer, was pregnant once again when she was widowed in 1758. Six months later she brought her twelfth child into the world.

In this long list of children, we are particularly interested in Johannes, who was born and baptized on December 26, 1751.

The child became none other than Saint Clement Maria Hofbauer, even though he was given the name Johannes at his baptism. We will soon explain why he was later called Clement. To avoid any confusion, we will continue to call him Clement or Clement Maria in this book, since he has gone down in history under this name.

At the time of Clement's birth, Empress Maria Theresa, wife of the German Emperor Franz I, governed the Hapsburg countries. One of her domains was Moravia, the home of our saint. Maria Theresa was a good mother to her own sixteen children and a beloved sovereign beloved to her subjects. The Hofbauer-Steer family must have also treasured the Hapsburgs; otherwise many of their children would not have been named after well-known Hapsburgs.

Clement Hofbauer was just five years old when the horrors of war visited his homeland. The rattle of sabers and the roar of cannons are not the best music for children's ears. Who does not know this? However, these years of suffering brought about by the Seven Years' War between Austria and Prussia ended in 1763.

Another event may have deeply marked Clement more than the slaughter of war. The boy was not yet seven when he lost his father, Paul Hofbauer, who died on July 26, 1758, at the age of forty-six-years-old.

Clement would never forget the day his father died. One scene in particular remained fixed in his memory. His mother took her son to a crucifix. Pointing to the image of the Savior, she said, "My child, from now on, this is your father. Be careful to follow the path that pleases him." Today a stone cross with an inscription commemorating this event has been erected in a field that once belonged to the Hofbauer family. Until the end of Clement's life, God would always be his father, one in whom he could always put his trust.

Now Clement's mother had to raise and support her children alone. A pious and intelligent woman, she put her faith in God. All his life, Clement spoke of her with the highest respect. He would often admit that after God, he owed everything good in his life mainly to his dear mother.

Other than these bare facts, we know very little of our saint's childhood. A telling anecdote about Clement has been handed down. When he was eight years old, he heard someone say, "I am

The birthplace of Saint Clement Maria Hofbauer, in southern Moravia. There is now a church named after Clement on the site.

killing time," and he wanted to know what the expression "killing time" meant. When his mother explained it to him, Clement was completely enraged. "If people have nothing to do, they should pray." Even in his old age, Hofbauer could still get angry about the expression "killing time."

In his younger years, Clement often helped his mother work in the fields. From this experience, Hofbauer was attached to solid peasant values and practical things—inclinations he held throughout his life.

Schooling was not obligatory in Moravia at the time. It is reported that Clement diligently attended the village school, and he often served as an altar boy in Tasswitz's village church, which was administered by the monks at Klosterbruck.

The young boy probably spent some time with his relatives in Budwitz, where he learned some Czech. This knowledge of the Bohemian language would be of great service to him later in life.

Undoubtedly, Clement felt the desire to become a priest very early. In order to prepare himself for the priesthood, young Hofbauer took Latin instruction from the priests, either in the Tasswitz rectory or in the Klosterbruck monastery. (Hofbauer's village of Tasswitz belonged to the monastery estates.) But it was to be the fate of our saint that he would have to spend half a lifetime struggling toward the realization of his clearly felt calling.

CHAPTER 2

Apprentice Baker and Student: 1767–circa 1774

B y the time Clement turned sixteen, the large Hofbauer family had dwindled even more. The father and seven brothers and sisters were already dead. Only four of Clement's siblings were still alive: three brothers, who had already left home, and his sister, Barbara. She had married in 1765 and had taken over the parental home and the butcher shop. So, Clement now lived alone with his mother in a rented apartment.

Mrs. Hofbauer would have gladly given her son the chance to pursue his studies, but she was too poor and simply was not in a position to provide the necessary money. For better or for worse, she was forced to send Clement into an apprenticeship. Clement thus quietly buried his heartfelt wish to become a priest.

Apprentice Butcher of Znaim

In 1767, young Clement left the village of his childhood to move to the small town of Znaim, a few kilometers from Tasswitz. There Clement began a three-year apprenticeship with master-baker Franz Dobsch. He began work there on May 31, as recorded in the guild registry. The Dobsch family treated him as one of their own, and the family atmosphere was often lighthearted. Here Clement probably learned to sing and read music—a talent he would use later as a singer in his liturgical and pastoral work.

The Premonstratensian Monastery at Klosterbruck. Hofbauer completed part of his studies here at the grammar school.

The young apprentice was liked by everyone, and he felt quite at home in the baker's family. Nevertheless, he did not feel comfortable within himself. He still dreamed of another profession in which he could "do great things for the glory of God."

Student at Klosterbruck

Klosterbruck was a six-hundred-year-old Premonstratensian monastery, situated a short half-hour away from Znaim. Before his three-year apprenticeship to Franz Dobsch had elapsed, Hofbauer came to work as a journeyman in the monastery's bakery.

At the same time, in the years 1770 to 1771, terrible suffering from famine and typhus raged over the land. The poor streamed to Klosterbruck and waited in droves at the gates for a piece of bread. Many died right there. Clement surely must have seen it all.

Klosterbruck also contained a grammar school with an enrollment of thirty boys. This school had been founded in the sixteenth century. The abbot at the time knew of Hofbauer's secret wish to study. As a result, he gave the young baker a lighter workload so that he could attend classes. Clement also became the monastery's refectorian, waiting tables at meals, and served as the abbot's private servant. These double duties did not come easily to Clement. They frequently prevented him from "giving himself to prayer as often as he wished."

Clement completed the four-year program, but could not continue his studies in Klosterbruck because the grammar school had only the lower grades. He also did not have the money to continue studying elsewhere. Thus Hofbauer found his bold plan to become a priest despite all obstacles thwarted once again.

A Great Decision

Still, this hopeless situation turned into a blessing for Clement, and became a watershed in his life. On one hand, Hofbauer wanted to follow God's calling faithfully; on the other hand, all doors to the priesthood appeared to be locked. In the midst of this dilemma, he could see only one way out. Clement made a momentous decision to follow the only path possible. He decided to follow his inner longing for a life dedicated to God. He wanted to "live in isolation completely united with God and so serve him." If he could not serve God as a priest, at least he would live as a hermit!

Clement was about twenty-four when he left the monastery at Klosterbruck to follow this path. We have very little information for 1775 to 1784, from Hofbauer's twenty-fifth to his thirty-third year. We know he led the life of a hermit for a long time and in different places, and that he undertook many long and difficult pilgrimages, especially to Rome. We also know that he worked temporarily as a baker in Vienna and that he tried desperately to continue his studies.

In the next two chapters, we shall show Clement Hofbauer in these two roles: first as a zealous pilgrim, and then as a solitary hermit.

Border marker on the road from Vienna to Rome. The marker reads: End of the Imperial Italian Postal and Main Commercial Road on the Lower Austrian Side.

CHAPTER 3

The Holy Pilgrim

C lement Hofbauer traveled an unusual amount in his life-time, usually on foot. Pilgrimages were in his blood. He made his first great pilgrimage to Rome as an eighteen-year-old baker's apprentice.

The Meaning of Pilgrimage

"They were strangers and foreigners on the earth....They are seeking a homeland....They desire a better country, that is, a heavenly country" (Hebrews 11:13–16). This passage expresses the essential meaning of pilgrimage.

Our life is like a journey, a constant voyage to our destination. Whoever undertakes a pilgrimage leaves home, braves the trials of the journey, and travels the path to a holy place. Thus going on a pilgrimage obviously expresses our journey to God. We journey to a shrine, to the holy goal of our pilgrimage. The place of pilgrimage, the shrine, thus becomes a symbol of heaven, to which we travel here on earth. This arduous state of "being on the road," this constantly renewed act of leaving, can be a sign of an internal process in the hearts of human beings: a return to God, to salvation through penance.

Consequently, pilgrimages are anything but tourism and world travel. They are a symbol of a way of life and faith of the individual, a symbol of the Christian path of penance. Hermits were therefore often zealous pilgrims.

Enthusiastic Pilgrim to Rome

Clement Hofbauer made pilgrimages to many famous shrines, but the goal of all his pilgrimages was always Rome. Time and again he was inexorably drawn to the city. Indeed, Clement Hofbauer would not have been Clement Hofbauer without Rome. His love of Rome and his loyalty to the Bishop of Rome would accompany him all his life. No one knows exactly how often he undertook the long and difficult journey to the south, but documents claim: "before 1779 already three times," "often," "thirteen times."[1] Whatever the number, these journeys were always penitential pilgrimages, and Clement usually traveled from Vienna to Rome with one or more like-minded friends.

Clement and his friends had to save money for the pilgrimage carefully. The difficult journey was made on foot and took a long time (about four hundred hours). They sweated so much in the heat "that they could have bathed in it." They often slept outdoors. Clement would mark a circle on the ground with his staff and surrender himself to the protection of the apostles. Then he would lay down on the ground inside the circle and sleep the sleep of the just.

When the pilgrims finally arrived in Rome, "they made their devotions, visited the churches, and returned to the fatherland with renewed faith."

Prickly Adventures

On one trip to Rome, Clement and his friends were very tired. Suddenly, they saw before them a brightly lit house. Finally, they thought, an inn! With glad hearts and a quicker pace, they came closer. Inside, there appeared to be a party going on in full swing—loud music and boisterous laughter, as at a wedding reception. The pilgrims opened the door. What—what had happened? No one was in the house. It was dark and deathly quiet. A ghost, they thought. Quickly, the pilgrims left the haunted house.

On another occasion, also in Italy, a large dog came charging at the travelers. He wanted to attack Clement's companion. Clement recited the psalm, "Whoever dwells in the protection of the

Clement Maria Hofbauer visited Altötting, the famous Bavarian shrine, many times as a pilgrim (MH XII 26, 156). In the vault of the shrine is a votive statue, a kind of monstrance, underneath which Clement Maria Hofbauer is depicted as a pilgrim with a rosary, knapsack, and walking staff.

Almighty, may say to God: 'You are my refuge and my castle, Lord, whom I trust.'" By the time he finished this prayer, behold— the animal had disappeared. On this occasion, Clement said to his trembling friend, "My mother taught me to recite that psalm in case of danger."

Another time, the pilgrims were close to Rome. Night descended faster than expected. Looking for shelter, the pilgrims came across an isolated inn and entered. They were overcome with an anxious feeling. Everything seemed so suspicious. The innkeeper, a savage-looking man, spoke quietly with his other patrons about the newly arrived quests. Hofbauer's companions refused to spend the night, so Clement sent his two friends outside. He remained. While Clement was trying to pay his bill and take his leave, the innkeeper grabbed him and tried to restrain him by force. The strong young baker tore himself from the hands of the fiend and stumbled out into the night. Clement and his friends then hid. Shivers ran up and down their spines as several men stormed out of the inn with lanterns and large dogs. The dogs' wild barking echoed throughout the valley. The pilgrims kept quiet as mice until everything calmed down. Then they groped their way forward under cover of the sinister darkness.[2]

Clement's Strange Adventure

Many saints have a rare talent for adventure. The beginning of this adventure of Clement's resembles a comedy, the end resembles a detective novel. At the time, Clement was twenty-five years old. He wore a brown cowl and looked like a Capuchin friar. He was taking part in a pilgrimage to Mariazell dressed in this hermit garb. The rest of the pilgrims knew and trusted Clement, including Klara Kurzmann—an eighteen-year-old girl who told him of her wish to become a nun. This goal, however, was impossible in antireligious Austria. With remarkable shortsightedness and naiveté, the hermit Hofbauer offered to help Klara.

Clement then goes as a pilgrim to Rome. Two candidates for religious life join the experienced pilgrim Hofbauer, along with Klara Kurzmann. Clement suggests to Klara that she join a foreign convent, far away from the antireligious climate of Austria.

Klara gratefully goes along with this plan. Since she does not have a passport, Clement advises the girl to dress in men's clothing so that she will not be so obvious on the journey. No sooner was it suggested, and Klara was outfitted in men's garb. Klara plays her role perfectly, that is, until the pilgrims arrive in Rome.

Once there, Hofbauer takes the girl to some German-speaking nuns. There the story suddenly takes an unexpected turn. Klara is ashamed to admit to her disguise. The scene is embarrassing, especially for Hofbauer, who appears to be a prankster. He is fuming inside. An altercation ensues. But the fuss doesn't change Klara Kurzmann's mind. She stubbornly insists she is a man.

Thus, the alleged joker, Clement had no other choice but to take the stubborn woman back home with him across the Alps. In Carinthia, they ran out of money, and Clement suggested to his companion that they must now live off alms. The "candidate for the convent" refused emphatically to go begging. Hofbauer exploded and attacked her with a cane. Klara escaped and returned alone to Vienna.

In 1817, a diligent police detective came across this story and set the police machinery in motion. When interrogated, Klara confirmed the story. With luck, this affair was prevented from becoming an unpleasant episode for the then elderly Hofbauer. Proof of this narrow escape can be had by reading the police records.

But Clement was cured. From then on, he never let himself get mixed up in similar adventures. After the unfortunate outcome of his efforts to help a young woman, he would joke, "I thank God that I am not a woman and that I have no wife."

Pius VII (1800–1823). Barnabus Chiaramonti was Bishop of Tivoli (1782–1785). He took in the young Hofbauer as a hermit there. As pope, he became Hofbauer's patron and protector.

CHAPTER 4

Clement's Life As a Hermit: Whim or Calling?

H ofbauer left the monastery at Klosterbruck around 1774 to become a hermit. He became both a pilgrim and hermit at about the same time. What a strange combination! As a pilgrim he traveled for months at a time through the world; as a hermit he removed himself from the world in order to unite himself more easily in solitude to the person of the Savior.

We know that Clement Hofbauer lived for long periods as a hermit at different places in his homeland, as well as in Tivoli near Rome. Despite extensive research, it is still impossible to determine the chronology and duration of his stays in various hermitages. Many unsolved riddles and unanswered questions remain. Since the appropriate documents regarding this period of Clement's life are missing, for the moment we must rely on assumptions. More important, however, than the creation of a clear chronology of Clement's days as a hermit is our knowledge of what Clement actually intended to accomplish with his life of solitude.

The Life of a Hermit: An Ideal

Doubtless Hofbauer did not build hermitages in order to flee the worries of everyday life. Nor did he want to live in isolation as a lazy, harmless friend of nature, relying on donations for his keep. This was not Hofbauer's way. His interest was of another kind.

He chose this way of life because he felt himself called upon to follow the path of Christ more closely and because he hoped to achieve such an ideal.

So, what was the ideal of this form of Christian living as it was practiced in the eighteenth century in Clement Hofbauer's time? By greatly simplifying our explanation, we can look at it as having three essential characteristics.

Living With God in Solitude

Solitude is the preferred place for meeting God. The Bible, in fact, refers to a kind of "desert mysticism." In the solitude of the desert, a person can best find peace and his or her own true being, but also can experience the protection of God and the intimacy of His presence. In the endless, uninhabited (both real and metaphorical) sand dunes, all the usual securities fall away. The experience of loneliness makes a solitary realize that he or she can only rely on God now. This makes for humility and at the same time for confidence.

The experiences that arise from solitude are what make a real hermit—one who withdraws from the hustle and bustle of the world in order to turn one's eyes only to God in prayer. In this isolation, the hermit becomes less distracted and can more easily experience the friendship of God. In the eighteenth century, hermits were viewed as persons of peace and prayer. They were not allowed to accept guests into the hermitage and were allowed only four books: the Bible, a catechism, *The Imitation of Christ,* and the rules for hermits. An important part of a hermit's time was dedicated to contemplation and to the reading of the Scriptures. They were supposed to live united with God—free from everything, free for God.

For Clement Hofbauer, the time spent as a hermit was the novitiate of his life. As an old man, decades later, he would stroll through the noisy metropolis with half-closed eyes, intensely absorbed in God. Trusted friends who knew him best describe him as a "quiet and prayerful man," as a "man of prayer." Prayer was his "main occupation…the food and drink of his heart….His soul was always in the presence of God." And he "was always looking within." Later Hofbauer would get even his theological knowledge and the topics for his sermons mainly from the Bible, the catechism, and church history. Hofbauer had his own method of preaching until the end of his life. Deep in prayer, he would contemplate a Bible passage, then he would preach what he had learned with such conviction that the listeners were irresistibly carried away with him.

Living in Scriptural Poverty

Poverty, the second characteristic of the hermit's life is biblical through and through: "Blessed are the poor in spirit, for theirs is the kingdom of heaven" (Matthew 5:3). In a world which does not correspond to the Bible, human possessions, acts, accomplishments, and glories have great value. The life of a hermit is a radical attempt to take the words of Christ seriously. Part of the ideal of the hermit is to be a penitent, to kill pride and the hunger for possessions, to live in poverty and uncertainty and thus to entrust oneself to the care of the heavenly Father. There must be nothing superfluous in the hermitage. One needs a table, a chair, a strawbed, and a wool blanket: nothing more!

This separation from possessions was in no way contempt for earthly things. Quite the contrary, the hermit was supposed to love nature. Thus hermitages were often built in very beautiful places. Zacharias Werner reports on the hermit Hofbauer: "Thus you moved into the quiet of the forest, in order to study God from the living book." Although hermits were allowed to accept charity, they were not to live from begging, but rather to sustain themselves through the work of their hands and from the fruits of "the earth, our mother." They were supposed to tend a garden or work at a craft.

The years that Hofbauer spent as a hermit made a lasting impression on him. Yes, his entire life is a living illustration of this hermit-spirituality, even though he loved beautiful things (music, liturgy, art, for example). He lived precariously and freed from all unnecessary things. Whenever, in the course of his stormy life, all human security disappeared, then he relied even more as a child on God alone. He begged for others, and he often fed others with the fruits of his manual labor.

Living Within and Outside the Church

There were a great many hermits in the eighteenth century and this Christian way of life was recognized by the Church in many places. As a religious vocation, it had several similarities with the religious orders. The applicant was approved as a hermit after having been tested by the bishop. He received a new name, just as one who joins an order does. Hofbauer was originally called Johannes (John). As a hermit he received the name of Clement from the bishop. Hofbauer kept this hermit-name until his death. He always signed his letters Clement, Clement Maria, or Johannes Clement.

He also wore the clothes of a hermit: a belt, cowl, and a long rosary. A police report states that Hofbauer was "dressed as a Capuchin," indicating that he was a member of the Third Order of Saint Francis when he lived as a hermit.

Some hermits took vows, and that appears to have been the case with Hofbauer. This conclusion is derived from some of his own accounts. In an official report in 1777, Hofbauer writes that he entered the "Institute" near Rome and there he took the vows in 1778. This supports the statements of another report from 1800 wherein Clement maintains that he took his vows twenty-three years earlier—around 1777 or 1778.

Since the profession of hermit was a clerical profession, usually some service to the church was connected to it. Hermitages were often located near popular shrines, and, in many cases, the hermits undertook the role of sacristan. They were also assigned other duties: visiting the sick, administering to the poor, giving religious instruction, and so on. The "hermit" Clement Hofbauer studied catechism in Vienna in 1780, because as a hermit he had to give instruction in the faith.

Also in regard to this third aspect of the hermit ideal, the time Hofbauer spent as a hermit became his life's preparation, and perhaps accounts for one of his most noteworthy characteristics—his love of the Church. Perhaps he gained his feeling for the famous "perpetual mission" and for the beautiful decoration of liturgical spaces from the shrines where he had lived as a hermit.

All these aspects of life as a hermit in the eighteenth century influenced the later work of our saint and also help us to better understand Clement Hofbauer. Now we wish to accompany him further on his life's journey.

A Hermit in His Homeland

Once the twenty-four-year-old Clement had decided to become a hermit, he had to build himself a hermitage. About a half-hour from his hometown of Tasswitz lies the town of Mühlfrauen. This neighboring village was especially famous at that time because of its beautiful Church of the Scourged Redeemer. As a child, Hofbauer may have often made the pilgrimage to Mühlfrauen.

Close by, on the other side of the valley Thaya, lies a forest, the Pölzerwald. Clement Hofbauer inherited half a piece of land there. With his brother's help, he built a hermitage on this spot.

The new hermit soon gained a good reputation. A witness reports: "The pilgrims to Mühlfrauen visited the hermit. They brought him food. For his part, he gave religious instruction and gave out small crosses." Hermit and missionary would be two lifelong characteristics of our saint.

The hermit Clement would—as was the custom at the time—carry a heavy wooden cross from his cell in the Poelz Forest to the Church of the Scourged Redeemer in Mühlfrauen. He did this as an act of penance. The people gave him the name "Cross-bearer" or "Cross-dragger." He would remain a penitent and cross-bearer his entire life.

The length of time that the hermit Clement Hofbauer lived in Mühlfrauen cannot be determined with certainty.[1] The spirit of the age and the government of the day were not well-disposed toward monasteries or hermitages. The regulations and laws imposed on religious practice by the government became more and more draconian. Clement had to abandon his life as a hermit and leave his hermitage. He moved to Vienna where he found work in the bakery *Zur eisernen Birne* (The Iron Pear) across from the Ursuline convent. On Sundays and feast days he served at Mass in St. Stephen's Cathedral and in the Church of the Savior.

His new employer, master-baker Weyrig, was satisfied with his journeyman; otherwise he would not have offered him his

daughter's hand in marriage. The offer would have been an entic-
ing one to some. But it created a crisis for Clement who declined
this dream arrangement out of loyalty—because he felt himself
called to something else. With this decision he left his employ-
ment at The Iron Pear.

Hermit in His Chosen Home of Tivoli

A well-informed witness gave testimony during Hofbauer's canonization process that "his spirit was strongly attracted to the life
of the hermit." In September 1779, Clement applied for a vacant
hermitage near Vöttau, about thirty kilometers (eighteen miles)
north of Znaim. We do not know whether the provincial government approved this application. But we do know something else.

Around 1780, the measures against religious orders and hermits were drastically accelerated in Austria. In 1781 and 1782,
Joseph II suspended all hermit communities in Austria and out-
lawed hermits. Many hermits sought refuge in Rome or in other
Papal States. Such was the case for Clement Hofbauer and his
friend Peter Kunzmann.

Peter Kunzmann was a baker like Clement and only one year
older. They undertook pilgrimages to Rome together, the first time
in 1768. Now that hermits had been banned in Austria, "both
men decided to travel to Rome once again and to settle as hermits
in the Papal States." Kunzmann sold some articles of clothing and
some gilt buttons to raise the necessary money for the trip. Then
they began their journey and arrived happily in Rome "where
they made their devotions." From there they went to Tivoli to
request permission for their hermitage from the bishop.

Tivoli and the Madonna of Quintiliolo

At that time, Tivoli was a small town, about thirty kilometers
(eighteen miles) from Rome. Facing it stood a shrine set in a beautiful landscape. The people gave the church the name "Madonna
of Quintiliolo" because it was built on the marshlands owned by
the great general Quintilius Varus. Within the church was a cen-
turies-old miraculous image. Usually two or more hermits lived in

Quintiliolo at Tivoli near Rome.

the bordering hermitages as guardians of the shrine. The city of Tivoli and the Madonna of Quintiliolo are separated by the river Aniene (Anio). The solitude, the rustling of the olive trees, the roar of the water, the beautiful countryside, the ruins of old villas, made it the cemetery of an antique world. It was an ideal place to experience the presence of God.

Two Hermits of Tivoli

Clement had undoubtedly already visited Tivoli before he and his companion Kunzmann moved there from Vienna. The pilgrimage route from Austria to Rome had probably passed through Tivoli. Perhaps Hofbauer lived more than once as a hermit near the Madonna of Quintiliolo.

The two pilgrims Hofbauer and Kunzmann presented themselves to the bishop. Barnabas Chiaramonti, a Benedictine who later became Pope Pius VII, was Bishop of Tivoli from December 21, 1782, to February 14, 1785, so it may have been early in 1783 when they appeared before the bishop. He tested the two candidates. "He explained to them the burdens and duties of the hermit and tested them in their resolve. Since they remained steadfast in their decision, he gave them the habit, blessed them, and assigned them to a hermitage." Peter Kunzmann was given the hermit name of Emmanuel.

The presence of a hermit within a hermitage was usually temporary. Clement remained about six months. He "prayed and fasted much." Hofbauer was happy. Later, he would often tell his confidants about "what happy days he had spent in that solitude."

He would speak of his "very beloved hermitage of the Madonna of Quintiliolo." Shortly before his death he was very excited as he spoke of his former hermitage: "Children, if only you knew the beautiful area of Tivoli. There one can pray well, one is separated from the world and hence totally united with God."

Faithful and Trustworthy

This half-year in Tivoli was not wasted time. On the contrary, it was an essential part of the novitiate of the missionary Clement Hofbauer. In hindsight, this is easy for us to see. Through deep prayer undertaken there, Clement had prepared himself for his active missionary work. The life of a hermit was indeed not his

The old university in Vienna where Clement Hofbauer studied theology.

calling, but it was certainly a good preparation for his future apostolic work. In solitude God speaks to the soul: "I will lead you to the desert and will speak to your heart." Later, whenever Hofbauer was overwhelmed by his various projects, he would often recall his beloved Tivoli. There he sought to know the will of God, but eventually he sacrificed his deep longing for a life in solitude for a highly active life. Such statements are the golden keys to an understanding of Saint Clement Maria. Many years later Pater Hofbauer would write to his superior general: "If I wanted to follow my natural inclination and my desire, then above all else I would ask to be recalled to Italy. There I could live free from worldly cares and dedicate myself only to my eternal salvation, works of piety and devotion...in blessed peace and in the contemplation of divine things."

In the solitude of Tivoli near the Madonna of Quintiliolo, he had surely listened with special attention and a willing heart to the call and the will of God. People close to him confirm this: "After a while Hofbauer recognized the will of God more clearly, that he was not called to lead the life of a hermit, but rather that he was called to an active life." "The desire to continue his studies awakened in him," because he "felt within himself the incessant desire to become a priest." Therefore, he left the hermitage "without telling Father Emmanuel anything and returned to Vienna."[2] The apostle was stronger than the hermit.

We can only be amazed! How mysterious are the ways of Divine Providence! How strangely challenging the plans of God can be! A thirty-two-year-old man stands before the abyss. But he trusts in God. And he hopes against all hope. In this solitude and openness to God, he recognizes more clearly the will of God. Then he cannot hesitate any longer. He, entirely alone, without his companion, dares to step into the unknown, to step into the void.

CHAPTER 5

The University Student With the Catholic Nose

C lement "returned to Vienna in order to fulfill his higher calling, to continue his studies in fulfillment of his calling to the priesthood," according to a brief statement made by a confidant of our saint.

Friendships for Life

Much in a person's life can simply not be accomplished by his or her own efforts alone. Instead it is given to him. Even the life of a saint is essentially rooted in encounters with others. Clement Maria Hofbauer also grew from contact with others. In this sense, true friendships are gifts.

During his student days in Vienna, Clement made the most important friendship of his life—that with Father Niklaus Josef A. von Diessbach (1732–1798). Clement would write after his friend's death: "I was bound to him by an inner bond of friendship although he was much older than I." The same letter contains elements of a short biography of his friend. Diessbach came from an old aristocratic Swiss family, was raised a Calvinist, became a military officer, converted to Catholicism, and married a countess who died young. After the death of his wife, he gave his child into good care, renounced his military career, and became a Jesuit and a missionary. In Switzerland, Diessbach was called the

Apostle of the Alps. He came to Vienna in 1782. Before Christmas 1798, enemies of the Church attacked him and beat him so severely that he later died from his wounds. Hofbauer revered Diessbach as a truly apostolic man. He expressly wished to be buried in the cemetery of Maria-Enzersdorf because his friend Diessbach was buried there.

In 1778, Diessbach founded an organization called Christian Friendship (*Amicizia Christiana*) in Turin. This organization of priests and laity was secret in nature. The members signed "A.C." after their names, using the initials of their secret society. This brotherhood set for itself three goals: to further Church beliefs and religious life, to fight against the Enlightenment and state-churchism, and to distribute good books.

Diessbach probably founded this reform group in Vienna as early as 1782. Hofbauer was active in the Christian Friendship group in which he met men who would later become his greatest friends and patrons: Baron Josef von Penkler (1751–1830), Josef von Beroldingen (1738–1816), and others. After Diessbach's death, Ludwig Virginio (†1806) was in charge and the leader of the Christian Friendship in Vienna. Hofbauer maintained a lively correspondence with him as well. And Thaddeus Hübl, Hofbauer's most intimate friend and companion, must also have belonged to this group of reformers. Hübl uses the abbreviation A.C. in a letter as late as 1806. We may assume, therefore, without reservation that this group around Diessbach greatly influenced the thirty-two-year-old student Clement Hofbauer. Within this circle, he must have gotten many inspirations for his later missionary work.

Diessbach became a kind of father figure to Hofbauer for another reason as well. The aristocratic Swiss Jesuit Diessbach had personally known Alphonsus Liguori, the founder of the Redemptorist Congregation. Diessbach was a zealous disseminator of Liguori's writings in Turin and Vienna. There is every indication that Diessbach first introduced Clement to the writings of Saint Alphonsus Maria Liguori. In addition, the founder of the Christian Friendship group counted for something in Hofbauer's entrance into the Redemptorist Congregation.

People With Good Hearts

It was pouring rain outside. Three ladies were waiting out the end of the storm under the portal of St. Stephen's. At that point, Hofbauer came out of the cathedral. Ready to help, he asked the ladies if he could get them a cab. They gratefully accepted this offer and when they learned that he took the same way home, they invited him to ride along. During the trip they started up a conversation. Clement revealed to them that he had always wished to become a priest. A lack of money had prevented him from fulfilling this wish so far. The three ladies were in fact sisters of the von Maul family, and daughters of an aristocratic and rich court minister. They pledged Hofbauer their assistance, and they kept their word. Hofbauer remained grateful to his benefactrices his entire life.

Student Tribulations

It was not easy for Clement to take up his studies again at the age of thirty-two. He himself admitted: "I had to study every moment, I even sacrificed the nights. If I were in danger of falling asleep I would hold the book in one hand, the candle in the other and walk back and forth in my room—to stay awake and gain time."

But more than sleep, it was the atmosphere that reigned at the university that tried his spirit. It was the time of the Enlightenment and an exaggerated state-church ideology ruled in Austria (Josephinism). Many professors were obedient followers of the Enlightenment, and the teachers in the Faculty of Theology were no exception. Every day, students heard claims that contradicted the teachings of the Catholic Church.

One day, a painful incident occurred in a lecture hall at the university. A professor must have made strong statements against Church dogma. Clement who "had a Catholic nose" grew more and more incensed and then he exploded. Hofbauer called out in the middle of the lecture: "Professor, what you are saying here is no longer Catholic." The enraged student stood up and left the lecture hall. This event had repercussions, when, many years later,

St. Stephen's Cathedral in Vienna.

the two men met on the street in Vienna. The professor approached Hofbauer, stopped him and thanked him. During the conversation, the old teacher admitted that this incident had been humiliating yet beneficial for him.

It was during Hofbauer's university studies in Vienna that Emperor Joseph II ordered a reform of the universities according to the spirit of the Enlightenment. The study of theology became obligatory in the so-called general seminary courses. These courses were completely under the control of the state. This was too much for Hofbauer. He decided to continue his theology studies in Rome, as one document states, "in order to draw theological knowledge from a pure source." Elsewhere we read that he was disgusted by the lectures in Vienna because they were "rationalistic, completely un-Catholic, and unchristian."

Clement went on to Rome, and the journey will bring on the decisive turning point in Clement Hofbauer's life.

CHAPTER 6

The First Non-Italian Redemptorist: 1784-1785

I n Vienna, Hofbauer knew a fellow student named Thaddeus Hübl, who was from a poor family and who was nine years younger than he was. Both were of the same mind and were preparing themselves for the priesthood. During their university studies they were close friends. They remained inseparable in good times and bad until death.

Hofbauer had decided to undertake a pilgrimage to Rome in late summer of 1784 and, if possible, to continue his theology studies in the Eternal City. When he tried to convince his friend to move with him to Italy, Hübl protested: "I am sick and have no money." Clement responded: "I will get the travel money, and God will take care of the rest."

Hübl quickly recovered from his illness. The usual preparations for the journey were made, and in September Hofbauer and Hübl headed south across the Alps. Joseph II had proclaimed the famous Emigration Act on August 10, 1784, which declared that whoever entered a foreign monastery would face a severe penalty. Did our two travelers know this?

A Sign of Divine Providence

Upon their arrival in Rome, things fell into place. The pilgrims found accommodations near the church of St. Mary Major. One night, they agreed that the next morning they would go into the church whose bells they heard first. In the early morning, the monastery clock of San Giuliano rang. The two friends entered. After Mass, Clement asked an altar boy the name of this order. The boy answered, "They are Redemptorists," and immediately added, "You will become one of them, too." The two students stood there astounded. Clement thought a moment. To him, this strange answer appeared to be an invitation from God. The two men rang the bell at the monastery gate and stated that they wished to speak to the superior of the house. The sixty-year-old Father Landi appeared. Hofbauer and Hübl asked questions. They would like more information on the Redemptorist religious community.

And—Hofbauer immediately asked to be accepted into the Congregation. His friend Hübl hesitated. For him, this was all too surprising. He needed time to think. They exchanged bitter words. Clement spent the entire night in prayer. The next day everything was set: Hübl also decided to ask for acceptance into the Congregation of the Redemptorists.

Thus one can briefly summarize the two most decisive days in Hofbauer's life! This surprisingly fast decision to join the Redemptorists was, however, not a rash act caused by a child. A confidant of Hofbauer's admits that the prediction of the boy helped Hofbauer "come to a decision."[1]

The Congregation of the Redemptorists

At this time, the Redemptorist community was still very young, barely fifty years old. Alphonsus, the founder, was an exceptional man. A patrician's son, Alphonsus *de* Liguori, was very talented; at the age of sixteen he was both a doctor of law and a doctor of theology. After a brilliant legal career, the famous lawyer became a priest, pastor, and friend to the lower classes of the city of Naples, spending all of his energy in the service of the poorest of the poor. One day, Alphonsus collapsed. The doctors prescribed a holiday in the mountains. What he saw there broke his heart: the poverty and the spiritual devastation of the people in the countryside. Once again he felt the call of God. He decided to form a congregation "to proclaim the Gospel to the poorest and most abandoned."

Later, Alphonsus became a bishop. He used his rich talents and artistic abilities entirely in the service of pastoral work. As a religious writer and moral theologian, he wrote over one hundred books, which later enjoyed an unusual number of new editions and reprints. As a musician, he composed religious songs, some of which are still popular today. After a fruitful and holy life, the founder of the Redemptorists died in 1787 at the age of the ninety-one.

His community was given the name of the Congregation of the Most Holy Redeemer (Redemptorists, that is to say, the Redeemer's Missionaries). According to the wishes of the founder, this order was to be a missionary one—followers of Christ, preachers of the Gospel, servants of the poor. These three points summarize the ideals of the Redemptorists.

Such a man as Alphonsus and such ideals must have inspired Clement Hofbauer and his student friend Thaddeus Hübl. Alphonsus Liguori was indeed a fateful figure for Hofbauer, for without the Saint of Naples, the Apostle of Vienna, as we know him, would have been impossible.

Clement Hofbauer—A Redemptorist

The two applicants moved into the house of the Redemptorists. As early as October 24, 1784, both men were vested in the garments of the Order. Thus began their novitiate, their probation period. Father Landi, their novice master, was a man who personally knew Alphonsus very well. He had also written a history of the Congregation. Certainly Father Landi taught his novices to love the Congregation and the spirit of its founder.

Besides a few amusing anecdotes, very little information from this probation period has survived. Clement could occasionally become frustrated over cultural differences. The Italian novices took a change of clothes with them, even on a two-hour hike. When he observed these complicated preparations, he became disgusted. He told the master of novices: "Your Reverence, just as you see me here, with one shirt, one jacket, pants, a hat and a cane, I traveled two hundred miles without damaging my health. And here one makes such preparations for a two-hour hike!"

By his own admission, hunger was his greatest problem. He

had brought a good appetite with him from the north. Sometimes he could not sleep for hunger.

On March 19, 1785, the first non-Italian Redemptorists, Clement Hofbauer along with Thaddeus Hübl, pronounced their vows in the Congregation. Father Superior General Francesco de Paola accepted their vows in the monastery of Rome. Immediately afterward, the two were sent to the Redemptorist house of studies in Frosinone in the southern part of the Papal States.

Finally At His Goal

Both men, surprisingly, were ordained priests ten days later. No book records what Clement Hofbauer experienced inside as he knelt before the bishop on March 29, 1785, and was ordained a priest. For a quarter of a century he had waited for the day, struggled for this hour of consecration, prayed for this grace. After an obstacle course of zigzags—finally he became a priest! No letter, no report, betrays to us something of his inner feelings on his ordination day, but we can easily imagine his grateful joy.

His happiness, however, was only internal. On the outside, everything was quite matter of fact. After the ordination, which our two friends probably received in the cathedral of Alatri, they had to march home to the monastery of Frosinone on foot. The weather was terrible, and there was no celebration. Father Hübl had to read aloud at table, and Father Hofbauer had to serve the food. This was strange recognition for the newly ordained priests.

We may assume that Hofbauer's mother was informed of her son's ordination in good time. There is also no record of how much this brave woman prayed for her son and suffered for him. Most likely this March 29 was a high point in her life. A few weeks later, on June 3, God called her home to him.

The two priests Hofbauer and Hübl remained in the Redemptorist monastery of Frosinone until the fall. They were supposed to complete their novitiate and their theology studies there. At the same time, they were to get to know better the spirit and life of the Congregation in the Redemptorist house of studies.

Though Clement never met the founder of the Congregation personally, he chose the Neapolitan missionary Alphonsus Liguori as his example and his role model. He was interested in Liguori's life and work and especially in his writings. His thirst for knowledge was insatiable in this regard and was sustained to the end of his life. This persistent attachment to Alphonsus Liguori's writings were proof enough that Clement loved the Redemptorist Congregation and its founder very much.

CHAPTER 7

Courage! God Is in Charge

Exactly half of Clement Hofbauer's life had passed by the time he was ordained a priest. They were a stormy thirty-four years. If we look back upon this part of our saint's life, then we must agree with Hofbauer's contemporaries who characterized his life as "a thornbush" and "a miracle." It appears to us in fact like a strange combination of zigzags, confusions, and Divine Providence.

"God can also write straight with crooked lines," a proverb says. First, we see Clement as the son of a farmer, working in the fields, next as an apprentice kneading dough at the trough, then as a servant, a grammar-school student, hermit, baker, pilgrim, university student, and finally as a Redemptorist and a priest. These twisted paths—which we call detours—were, for God, the straight roads to Clement's goal. Later Clement would write in a letter what may be thought of as a résumé of his first thirty-four years: "Courage! God is in charge."

Some profound influences, like deep rivers, flowed together to nourish Clement and mark him: the faithful and long-suffering parents in a farming village; the international character of this hybrid of Czech and German families from the border area of southern Moravia; the practical talents of a baker and part-time student; the seemingly contradictory lives of a hermit and a pilgrim; the love of Rome and its bishop (so much so that he went to Tivoli near Rome, had his novitiate in Rome, and was devoted to the pope and to his nuncios); the Christian Friendship group around Diessbach and Penkler; the long years of struggle toward his clearly recognized vocation to follow the will of God; and his contact with the Scriptures and the Congregation of Saint Alphonsus.

Clement completed a very short novitiate with the Redemptorists. But the hard school of life with its various activities and experiences was nothing other than a novitiate stretching out over thirty-four years. This long probation period was a great preparation for his actual calling—that of a missionary. Jesus "called to him those whom he wanted, and they came to him." He wanted to have them near him and "to be sent out to proclaim the message" (Mark 3:16). The life of John Clement Maria Hofbauer is a living illustration of this biblical passage. As a hermit with a new name taken from a martyred bishop, Clement retreated into solitude in order "to be with God." There he gave the right importance to silence and prayer. As a pilgrim he traveled to other countries, to other people. Already there was something universal about him.

Toward Christ—Toward His People

The strength of his calling and his intimate union with God had well prepared him for the daring step, in 1785, of joining the Redemptorists. In the fall of 1785, the superior general called the two German Redemptorists from Frosinone to Rome. He wanted to discuss with them the realization of their shared plans. Hofbauer and Hübl were supposed to return to their homeland with a bold task: to try to plant the Redemptorist Congregation north of the Alps. It is amazing that the superior general entrusted this mission to the new priests who only shortly before had come into contact with the Redemptorists!

Rome—the city of his desires, of his pilgrimages, of his novitiate—now became the place of Hofbauer's missionary send-off. The Eternal City was now, and would always remain, the linchpin in his life. Rome concludes the exciting first half of Hofbauer's life; the second half would be even more dramatic and adventurous.

Part Two

Clement in Warsaw
1787–1808

CHAPTER 8

Off to the North
1785–1787

The two new priests, Hofbauer and Hübl, headed north in October 1785. They were sent into uncertainty without money or an exact destination. Their path took them first to the shrine at Loreto and then through the Tyrol to Vienna.

Upon their arrival in the Imperial City, they brought the papal nuncio a letter of recommendation from the Dean of the College of Cardinals. Then they took a course for catechists at the normal school at St. Anna. The course consisted of lectures and practical exercises.

The two Redemptorists soon realized that establishing a new monastery in Vienna or Austria was unthinkable. Emperor Joseph II had already closed more than eight hundred monasteries in his realm.

Moreover, the Redemptorists did not seem to fit in with the times. Alphonsus Liguori had founded his Congregation so that its members would preach the Gospel to the poorest of the poor, primarily in the form of popular missions. But it was precisely these types of missions that were completely banned in Austria at that time.

The leadership in Rome followed Hofbauer and Hübl's efforts in Vienna with great interest and concern. Father de Paola wrote Clement on February 7, 1786, and again on June 10, that he should return to Italy if in fact he did not believe anything positive could be achieved. If, however, a real chance existed to begin a foundation in Austria, Germany, or another northern country, then he was prepared, as superior general, to send priests from Italy.

We are poorly informed regarding Hofbauer's further efforts, negotiations, plans, and dreams. In May, our friends made a pilgrimage to Mariazell, Austria's most famous shrine. We can only imagine the fervor with which they celebrated the Eucharist there and prayed to the Queen of Apostles. They then left Vienna in October, planning to travel north through Poland to Russian Poland or Stralsund in Swedish-Pommerania.

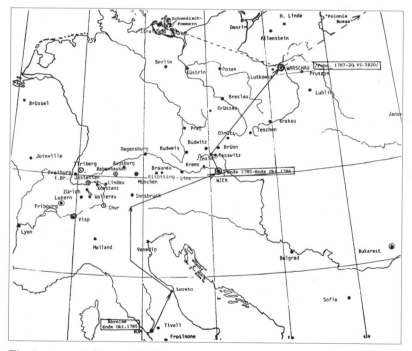

The journey of Clement Hofbauer and Thaddeus Hübl from Rome to Warsaw via Vienna, which began at the end of October 1785 and lasted until February 1787, with a stay in Vienna.

A Fairy-Tale Reunion

Hofbauer and Hübl arrive at the Danube and see a very poorly dressed hermit. They move closer. What? Is it possible? Clement doesn't believe his eyes. Isn't that...? It is! Emmanuel Kunzmann! The three friends greet one another enthusiastically. They have so much to tell. Memories of shared pilgrimages to Rome are rekindled. Clement and Hübl explain that they are now priests. Emmanuel kneels down and asks for their blessing. Then they share their plans with one another. Kunzmann wants to undertake a pilgrimage to the sepulcher of the Three Holy Magi in Cologne. Then he wants to travel to Italy again and continue the life of a hermit. But he admits that his strength has diminished and he is always ill. He can no longer do hard physical work.

Clement Hofbauer has compassion for his fellow hermit from Tivoli, the man with whom he had shared many pilgrimages. He invites Emmanuel to come with him and Hübl to Warsaw. Kunzmann accepts gladly and shows interest in joining the Congregation of the Redemptorists. Hofbauer promises to have him admitted by the General Government in Rome. Thus, Emmanuel, the old rover, becomes the first Redemptorist brother north of the Alps.

This episode had repercussions that are indicative of the spirit of the times. A snoop must have overhead all these happy plans. The newspaper *Wiener Kirchenzeitung* prominently displayed this story: "A couple of Roman ex-Jesuits...arrived here. ...They have also enlisted people; and although we do not know the number of their recruits, we can name one of them. His name is Peter Kunzmann...a much traveled journeyman baker....When he was recruited, he was given the habit of the order....They gave him the name Emmanuel and took him with them to Mohilow."

Home Again in Tasswitz

Hofbauer continued on his way through Hollabrunn to Znaim with the two companions of his youth and travels. As they were marching along the streets that had turned to mud in the rain, a carriage suddenly stopped. The schoolmaster from Retz took pity on these soaked monks. He invited them to climb aboard and to spend the night at his house.

On October 14, 1786, Clement wrote the hospitable teacher and his family a thank-you note and enclosed a souvenir from Loreto. This note is the first letter of the saint that has survived to our times. It was kept in the teacher's family like a rare treasure. Many years later, the wife would admit: "This letter brought a blessing into our house."

In the village of Tasswitz, where Hofbauer had spent his childhood, he visited relatives and went to see his mother's grave. What sadness he must have felt in the cemetery of Tasswitz!

Then Hofbauer and his companions traveled further. It was a harsh winter, and the three Redemptorists made slow and difficult progress. Their journey to Warsaw took an entire four months, for they did not arrive in the Polish capital until February 1787.

CHAPTER 9

The Beginning in Warsaw

At the end of the eighteenth century, Warsaw was a medium-sized city. The population of the city fluctuated greatly because of the ravages of war. From 1787 until 1792, the population climbed from 98,000 to 120,000. Then the number fell quickly again. In 1796, Warsaw had only 66,400 inhabitants: 54,000 Catholics, 6,000 Protestants, and 4,600 Jews.

Our trio arrived during a wintry February in 1787. They were soon received by the papal nuncio, Ferdinand Maria Saluzzo. This prelate, himself a Neapolitan, was a personal friend of Bishop Alphonsus Liguori. He was considered a great patron of the Redemptorists.

The wheels of intrigue were set in motion as soon as rumors spread of the arrival of the new priests in Warsaw. Some wanted to keep the missionaries in the city; others wanted to send them on their way as soon as possible.

St. Benno

There was in Warsaw a religious foundation dating from 1623. The purpose and goal of this monastery was to house poor travelers, to nurse sick strangers, and to care for non-Polish orphans. This charitable organization was run by the Confraternity of St. Benno.

The majority of foreigners living in Warsaw were Germans. Thus the leadership of this fraternity was in their hands. For that reason, St. Benno, the church of the brotherhood, was at the same time the national church of the Germans in Warsaw.

Earlier, the Jesuits had been active at this foundation, whose church had fallen into neglect after the Society of Jesus was suppressed in 1773. The neighboring buildings had collapsed. The Confraternity of St. Benno searched in vain for suitable priests to take over the church and for suitable personnel to breathe life into the school for poor German children. The newly arrived German-speaking Redemptorists were the answer to their prayers.

The board of directors of the Confraternity came to Father Hofbauer with a plan. They asked him to take over the church and school of St. Benno. They also enlisted the help of the papal nuncio Saluzzo. He urged the priests to remain temporarily in Warsaw. The King himself, Stanislaus II, interceded, and called them to a personal audience. He completely forbade them to leave the city. An official document reads: "As Germans, they were welcomed by the German Catholic community and, finally, after many refusals, they gave up their travel plans and took over the education and the administration of the school and Institute established by the Confraternity of St. Benno."

Hofbauer, therefore, remained in Warsaw temporarily. The board of the Confraternity of St. Benno, the nuncio in Warsaw, and Clement himself sent letters to the superior general in Rome. On May 24 and again on May 31, Father Francis de Paola gave Clement and his colleagues permission to remain for one year or longer in Warsaw.

Every Beginning Is Difficult

What Hofbauer now undertook borders on insanity—the insanity of a saint! In the beginning, the three sons of Alphonsus occupied a damp room near the former Jesuit church. Water ran down the walls. The entire furnishings consisted of a table and some chairs. They had no beds, so during the first few nights, two of them lay down on the table, while the third made himself comfortable in a chair.

Brother Emmanuel Kunzmann took over the kitchen, even though he did not know the first thing about cooking. Since they did not have the necessary utensils, Emmanuel carved wooden spoons. The rest of the kitchen equipment was borrowed from some good-hearted people. Their entire petty cash was a mere two or three tallers.

During the first few years, they suffered more from the hostile attitude of various influential groups than from financial want. In 1772, the Prussians, allied with the Russians and the Austrians, had annexed part of Poland. Is it any wonder, then, that the Poles despised the Germans? Hofbauer wrote to Vienna in January 1788: "We are hated here because we are Germans."

Moreover, during those years, a great deal of hatred and hysteria was directed toward the Jesuits in many places. After the dissolution of the Society of Jesus, some people saw Jesuits in disguise everywhere. Hofbauer himself was attacked regularly because people suspected him of being a "Roman ex-Jesuit." The Bennonites, as the Redemptorists were called in Warsaw, encountered resistance and rejection from many different quarters. They were held up to ridicule by actors on the stage. On the streets they were cursed as Germans, as Jesuits, as Lutherans, or as religious fanatics.

Difficult Times

What Hofbauer and his confreres were able to achieve in Warsaw in twenty years can be seen as almost miraculous. Their accomplishments can only be fully appreciated when examined against the dark shadows of the historical background. These times, indeed, were very bad. A few images, a few dates, and a few main points should suffice to show the extent of their achievements and the nature of the obstacles they faced.

1787: Hofbauer arrives in Warsaw. Poland is still a monarchy. The Prussians, Russians, and Hapsburgs had already taken part of the country from King Stanislaus fifteen years earlier in 1772–1773 when the first partition of Poland occurred.

1793: Russia and Prussia again steal another large piece from what remains of Poland's homeland. This second partition of the king-

St. Benno in Warsaw
around 1787 (seen from
the Vistula River).

dom inflames hatreds and awakens the will to resistance among
Polish patriots. The freedom fighters rise up against their foreign
masters in 1794. At first, the resistance movement was successful. In Warsaw, fierce fighting begins. Many lives are lost in bitter
street fights. Bloody riots erupt during Holy Week. Soon squares
and alleys are littered with the dead. Even on Easter Sunday, Russian prisoners are systematically butchered by Polish freedom fighters although these prisoners kneel with hands clasped to beg for
mercy.

    It does not take long for the fortunes of war to turn. In the
countryside, the Polish rebels are bloodily defeated. Weeks pass.
One day, an even more terrible calamity descends upon the city.
Russian troops begin their approach to Warsaw. Marshall Suvorov
takes the suburb of Praha in a bold stroke. The Russian officers
lose control of their men. Foaming with rage, they massacre everyone in their path.

On December 29, 1794, Clement writes his superior general: "We were thrown into great fear by terrible turns of fate....When the city of Praha was taken, 16,000 people—men, women and children—were massacred. We had to witness these horrible scenes since they took place in front of our house. Only the Vistula separates our house from that suburb which is right on the river bank."

1795: The Kingdom of Poland is dissolved, and its king must abdicate on November 25. Russia, Prussia, and the Hapsburgs divide Poland among themselves. (This becomes known as the Third Partition of Poland.) The capital is promised to Prussia which takes over the city in 1796. Warsaw and consequently St. Benno remain under a Protestant, antireligious government for a full decade.

1807: After the Battle of Jena, the French march into Warsaw on January 2, 1807. In the peace treaty of Tilsit, which was signed on July 21, Napoleon gives "The Duchy of Warsaw" to his puppet, the King of Saxony. The great Corsican allows the Bennonites to be driven from Warsaw in 1808.

That is the historical context in which we must view the activities at St. Benno from 1787 to 1808. At this very same time, Europe is rocked by the French Revolution and by Napoleon's devastating military campaigns, which bring fear, tears, and terror along with them. As well, the spiritual turbulence during this time of the Enlightenment and Freemasonry is no less far-reaching. Naturally, all this tumult leaves behind clear marks on the Church, for there was much mischief inside this institution as well. Inevitably, the clergy were also divided by events and by the conflicts of the times. Hofbauer's shocking descriptions of religious and moral life during this time are hardly exaggerated.

For two decades, St. Benno's in Warsaw was the field of activity for Hofbauer and his confreres. The following chapters will describe the apostolate of our saint in his various activities during the "terrible times" from 1787 to 1808.

CHAPTER 10

Missionary to Neglected Youth

At the center of the apostolate of the missionary stood the person seen as a whole, especially the poor person. Thus Hofbauer saw the education of neglected youth as an eminently missionary task.

Schools of St. Benno

Without financial means and, in the beginning, with only two colleagues, Clement actually founded an orphanage and a school for the poor in Poland's capital. Later, as the numbers in the community grew, he founded a Latin school and a school for industrial arts.

School for the Poor

Hofbauer took over the school for the poor at St. Benno shortly after his arrival in Warsaw. At the start, he could accept 100 children—and soon 200. He held three classes for the boys and three for the girls. The number of boys varied greatly during those years: 152, 256, 268, 276. As a rule, there were fewer girls than boys. Thus the school for the poor numbered on average between 400 and 500 children.

The classes were free and open to children of German, Polish, and Russian parents. Boys and girls of other confessions were accepted without objection, as long as they were children of the lower classes, orphans, or abandoned. Being poor was apparently the only condition for entry.

Although there were good schools in Poland's capital, St. Benno's was the only school of this kind in all of Warsaw. The most important subjects were reading and writing in German and Polish, as well as arithmetic, religion, history, and geography.

The Latin School

One has always been able to exploit and push around the uneducated and ignorant poor. Father Hofbauer wanted to offer his poor pupils a chance for advancement. Thus he founded a kind of high school "for all those who want to study further." Perhaps his own experiences played a part in this decision.

Certain members of the upper class and some government groups were not at all supportive of Hofbauer's actions "because Latin is of no use whatsoever for this class of people."

The Industry and Trade School

Society needs qualified young people who form the world of the next generation. This was Hofbauer's conviction. He himself was once an apprentice, a working student, and a tradesperson. Clement was trying to ensure that the young children of the poor and the working class could also enter an apprenticeship and learn a trade. Thus he established a trade school for apprentices in Warsaw. Perhaps he engaged tradespeople for the workshops at St. Benno for this purpose. We are poorly informed about these training workshops; we must rely on assumptions. That the saint founded a trade and industrial school for girls in Warsaw is beyond doubt.

To his horror, Clement came to realize that many working-class young women in Warsaw were seduced early and fell into prostitution. Hofbauer wrote that in a city occupied by foreign troops there was hardly a street without a bordello. Women who had given in to prostitution worked there, not because they wanted to, but simply to earn a living. These exploited women were caught up in a vicious circle. Their own mothers were already sentenced to a life almost devoid of humanity; and their daughters had little chance to learn anything different on which to build their later lives. Clement could no longer watch as these young girls were drawn into the hellish circle. He had to help them find their dignity again by guiding them in ways that would make them able to earn an honest living. Hofbauer could not be shaken in his belief in the good in each person: "People are not that incorrigible! Most only go astray because they have never learned any better. A thousand experiences have convinced us of this." For this reason, Hofbauer founded an industrial school for neglected and imperiled girls. He found volunteers among the noble women and widows who gave classes in knitting, sewing, and cooking for free.

The Prussian government did agree that such a teaching institution was useful; but this particular school was a thorn in its flesh. Civil servants complained whenever they could, and inspectors objected to many things. Among their objections was their belief that it was absurd to take the young people to church several times daily. They believed that this waste of time came at the expense of the actual teaching of secular subjects. Additionally, other strange concerns were also raised. It was charged that the prolonged sitting required at this school "gave the bodies of the girls an extraordinary attractiveness." Instead of "red-cheeked girls," students soon became sickly, pitiable creatures. Finally, it was feared that these educated young ladies would break out of the lower class and assume a comfortable way of life. The first graduates of one Warsaw institution were proof of this.

Thus the southern Prussian government decided to close Clement's industrial school for girls in 1806. The justification stated rather delicately that it was inappropriate for a "girls' school to be run under the supervision of a men's monastery."

The Orphanage

From the very beginning, the Redemptorists had cared especially for neglected orphans and abandoned children at St. Benno. The boys were allowed to live there; they were fed and clothed. The girls, on the other hand, were put up with friendly families or in the homes of wealthy widows. After a while, the orphanage at St. Benno regularly housed between forty and sixty children. Clement himself often washed, combed hair, and picked lice from the orphans. "That was something!" he would later admit.

Job Placement and Counseling

True missionary work takes the specific individual seriously, wants to serve and benevolently accompany him or her through life. Perhaps it was just this pastoral journeying with the individual that was Clement's actual strength. This was already the case at St. Benno. The children were not simply left to themselves after leaving the school or orphanage. The Redemptorists continued to accompany them on their journeys through life. They endeavored to find good positions or suitable jobs for their charges. It goes without saying that the Bennonites were especially concerned about the religious and moral well-being of their former pupils.

Schools at St. Benno: A Twenty-Year Obstacle Course

The schools at St. Benno provided Hofbauer with a great deal of joy and more than a few worries. The available rooms for so many people were seriously narrow, unhealthy, and poorly furnished. There were often two dozen Redemptorists and forty orphaned boys housed in three buildings badly in need of renovations. In addition, hundreds of children were given classes there. Some priests had to live in the cellar. Occasionally, some of these rooms were commandeered by officers of the occupation army for their own quarters.

The Bennonites, as Saint Clement's group was often called, had to struggle with financial difficulties for twenty years. Clement was personally convinced that the continued existence of St. Benno was an uninterrupted miracle of Divine Providence. A large family of sixty or more people had to be fed daily. One time, the need for food was particularly great. As a result, some of the few pieces of furniture had to be sold. Clement often went begging for his orphans. Naturally, he was not always treated in a friendly manner; sometimes he was spitefully spurned. On one of these begging trips, a man screamed at him and spat in his face. Clement remained calm. He wiped the spit from his face and merely said, "So, that was for me. And now something for my orphans?" The man was so dumbfounded that he wordlessly pressed a tidy sum into the hands of the saint. Sometimes Hofbauer did not know where to turn. Then he went into the church, knocked on the tabernacle door, and pleaded, "Lord, help! Now is the time."

Besides material shortages, at the very beginning the schools and orphanage were also short of qualified personnel. Despite all the interference by the government, Hofbauer succeeded in gradually building up and training a respectable staff. Young Redemptorists who had been trained to be teachers amazed even the critical civil servants: "They show that they are bright and talented."

And the attitude of the government? Gradually, the Polish government learned to value the work of the Redemptorists in Warsaw. Eventually, they expressed great praise for Hofbauer and his schools. In 1793, the parliament of Grodno decided to massively increase the financial contributions for St. Benno. But then in 1796, a new government arrived. The southern Prussian government left no stone unturned in its attempts to sabotage the schools and orphanage. For a decade, official quarrels and spitefulness were the order of the day.

CHAPTER 11

The Perpetual Mission of St. Benno

The Redemptorist Clement Maria Hofbauer was without doubt a talented pastor and missionary. His concern for the Church inspired him with a rare force. In a short time, St. Benno became the religious education center and a focal point of Church life for all of Warsaw despite the hatred and "the incomprehensible rage against the Bennonites." Many comprehensive reports from varied sources make this point very clear.

The Daily Program

The pastoral work of St. Benno had been characterized at the time as a "perpetual mission." And indeed the offerings at this institution were surprisingly varied.

Beginning daily at six A.M., the mornings went as follows: a low Mass with hymns, a catechism lesson in Polish, a high Mass with plain chant, then a German and a Polish sermon, finally a solemn high Mass with musical accompaniment. In the afternoon, there was another German sermon. After that came a procession of the Most Holy Sacrament, then a sermon in Polish, the Way of the Cross, various devotions, and finally common evening prayer. This was the way it was every ordinary day of the year. In addition, sometimes there were addresses in French.

On Sundays and feast days, the mission day began at five a.m.

The Sunday program of observances was even fuller than that of the weekdays.

Preaching the Good News

Father Peter Blasucci,[1] the new superior general of the Redemptorists, believed he had to rein in Hofbauer's zeal. He suggested to Hofbauer that the faithful were being overfed with sermons. Clement replied that the superior general's fears were unfounded because religious ignorance in Warsaw was as great as the city's passionate hunger to alleviate this ignorance. In many churches, one heard only beautiful platitudes and empty phrases. In others, the faithful were prevented from receiving holy Communion by an exaggerated strictness based on the ideas of Jansenism. Because the priests at St. Benno's tried to preach the Gospel as Good News, the crowds were enormous. The church of St. Benno was much too small for the numbers of people it attracted. It held only about a thousand people.[2] That was the reason the Bennonites were forced to preach the Word of God four or five times a day. It was indeed the case that the house of God at St. Benno was full almost the entire day. As the Germans were going out one door, the Poles were already streaming in another.

At St. Benno's, however, one did not simply preach any old way. The priests structured their sermons thoroughly and systematically. During the course of a year, all the mysteries of the faith, the most important moral questions and the duties of each state in life were covered. The faithful were also supposed to be introduced to the Church calendar: thus the mysteries of salvation were preached according to the liturgical calendar. During Lent, for instance, emphasis was placed on conversion and the Easter sacraments. Holy Week was dedicated to the Passion of Christ.

There was also no shortage of variations in the form, structure, and content of the sermons. Three particular types of sermons were delivered at St. Benno: the catechetical instruction, the homily (a comment on a Bible passage and its application in the real lives of the faithful), and finally the thematic sermon (a certain subject or theme in faith or morals covered in detail). Besides Clement, Fathers Blumenau and Podgorski were the best known and most popular speakers. The eloquent Father Blumenau was considered the star preacher: "He could bring tears to people's eyes whenever and however he wanted. He was such a talented speaker that he could repeat in Polish whatever Hofbauer had just finished preaching in German."[3]

Celebrating the Faith

Hofbauer and his coworkers did not just preach about the faith. These tireless servants of the Word tried to celebrate the faith together with the people through beautiful liturgies, through processions and devotions at the Stations of the Cross, and through the sacraments. The whole individual was supposed to be addressed by such experiences and celebrations of faith. "It was as if a continuous celebration was taking place in the church." Such a compliment can only be appreciated in the context of the overly rational times of the Enlightenment.

One Mass during the day was said with special pomp and splendor, with music and singing. At least two-dozen violinists played. Even well-known Warsaw virtuosos volunteered in the orchestra. On the great feast days, the Bennonites held orchestral masses that often lasted over two hours. Usually a bishop or Father Hofbauer himself presided over the Eucharist. Music was carefully cultivated at St. Benno.[4] Clement bought an expensive musical instrument in Vienna for Warsaw, "the most beautiful one that you have ever seen in your lives." Once again the superior general in Rome believed he had to rein in his confrere in regard to music and singing. Hofbauer justified himself brilliantly: "This has nothing to do with pleasures for the ear but rather with praise of God. The more splendid the Mass, the better human beings can experience God. Through the harmony of the music, hearts and spirits can be raised to God and filled with piety.

The pomp and splendor in the church was supposed to give the Mass the character of a celebration. Clement would later admit: "The people hear more through their eyes than through their ears; they are captivated by their eyes. I experienced this in Warsaw." For this reason, he lit as many candles as he could. He dressed the priests so colorfully that it was a real joy. He decorated the altar. Only the most beautiful vestments were good enough for the Mass. The Bible occupied a place of honor. Clement succeeded in procuring an illustrated version of the Bible from Germany. He proudly wrote his colleagues in Warsaw that he was sending "a Bible with illustrations which were done in the finest monasteries....Perhaps there is no more beautiful Bible in any monastery in Poland."

This show of pomp and splendor was a determined antidote to the excess rationalism of the Enlightenment. This joyfulness in the faith as a reaction to the excessive severity of Jansenism was understood by the faithful. Many were thankful that they were allowed to come to St. Benno where "the most beautiful and most wonderful Masses in all of Warsaw" were celebrated.

But all this only served to exasperate the opponents of St. Benno. The civil servants in southern Prussia accused the Bennonites of grave crimes: the spreading of superstitions, extremism and fanaticism, and Catholic nonsense regarding the veneration of Mary. More than all the others, Clement Hofbauer was "by far the greatest fanatic." Official chicanery was the order of the day. When Hofbauer hung a holy picture in the church without the permission of the government, this act was blown up into a crime of treason.

Celebration of the Sacraments

The liturgy and the celebration of the sacraments are the highest forms of Gospel proclamation. The sacrament of penance was regarded as the focal point of pastoral work at St. Benno. After their personal morning prayers at 4:30 A.M., the priests heard confessions daily until well into the night. They only took a short break at midday. People came from all over to partake of the sacrament of penance. The confessionals were always besieged by long lines. The number of yearly Communions increased from 2,000 to over 140,000 in twenty years.

Popular Missions

This kind of extraordinary pastoral work was very dear to the Bennonites because of the history of the Redemptorist Congregation. In the beginning, Clement had no missionaries who were capable of preaching a mission in Polish in the rural parishes. The rural parishes were made up almost exclusively of Poles and in the city they were the majority. In 1801, Hofbauer reported to his superior general that he had been trying to gain permission from the government to hold missions in a parish church in Warsaw and other places for seven years. However, the southern Prussian government set draconian conditions. The first attempt at such an eight-day mission was undertaken by the Redemptorists in St. Benno itself. In 1801, they were allowed to hold their first great mission in Poland. Father Hübl and five confreres preached in three different parishes in the country. The success was overwhelming. Nearly 11,000 faithful came to the sacraments. Father Hübl gave out Communion for a full three hours on one day. The Bennonites did not take any money for these missions in the various parishes. As far as we know, Hofbauer never held such a mission himself.

Special Pastoral Works

St. Benno worked like a magnet. People of other faiths learned about the Catholic Church there. Many wished to join. The number of interested people was so great that they had to create separate classrooms for the Protestants and the Jews. One priest specialized in converting Jews, another in converting Protestants.

One pastoral undertaking of the Bennonites was particularly daring for the times. A priest gave classes and held days of meditation for women who had fallen into prostitution and for girls who were in danger of doing so. They were prepared for reentry into society.

Pastoral work had always been a great concern of Saint Alphonsus. Clement Hofbauer followed the example of the founder of his Congregation. The house of St. Benno was also apparently open to weak or psychologically disturbed priests. Even religious

"who needed to improve themselves" found refuge in the house
of the Bennonites.

CHAPTER 12

Hofbauer's Coworkers

C lement Maria Hofbauer, this "truly apostolic man," was indeed the heart and driving force of St. Benno. But he would not have been able to complete this great work alone. He had his colleagues, indeed many and very able colleagues.

Clement's Confreres

The little monastery of St. Benno had started small. First, there were only three residents: Clement Hofbauer, Thaddeus Hübl, and Brother Emmanuel Kunzmann. Soon afterward, a young candidate named Matthias Widhalm joined them from Vienna. We can assume that he had known Hofbauer in Vienna. Upon his arrival in the Polish capital, the applicant went to the church of St. Benno. There he was gripped by a sudden panic. He was just about to flee when Clement Hofbauer entered. All his fears dissolved after a brief conversation with the saint. Widhalm took his vows in the Congregation as Brother Matthias on August 25, 1790.

Others followed: the first Saxon, Karl Jestershein (1788), the first western Prussian, Adalbert Schröter (1792), the first Pole, Johannes Podgorski (1793), the first Frenchman, Joseph Passerat, along with three other of his countrymen (1796),[1] and the first Swiss, Johannes Appenzeller (1798). The number of St. Benno members grew noticeably. In 1799, the community already numbered twenty-five. During the twenty years from 1788 to 1808, sixty-five Redemptorists belonged to the community in Warsaw.

These colleagues were for the most part men of stature. Clement himself greatly praised them. "I can affirm with joy that I observe a great attachment to the Congregation among all my confreres." Almost all the priests were fluent in three languages. Father Hübl is supposed to have mastered seven languages. There were naturally also a number of difficult types. In particular, a psychologically ill member of the community gave Clement much trouble.

Theory and Practice

Alphonsus Liguori, the founder of the Congregation, believed that each priest must have a solid scholarly training. Hofbauer, as vicar general, also furthered the studies of his future priests and missionaries with all the means at his disposal. Students from St. Benno were always "the first and best prize winners" among the seminarians of Warsaw.

As a practical man, Hofbauer did not wish to convey only theoretical knowledge to his clerics. He tried rather to train the young priests to be practical missionaries through pastoral activity and practice. That is why the Redemptorist novices and clerics had to explain the catechism in church, lead the choir, present the readings, lead the Stations of the Cross, and direct the people in their examination of conscience, and so on. Hofbauer wrote, "This way they gain more confidence."

A Lay Elite: the Oblates

Hofbauer's missionary service was directed entirely to the conversion of the individual, to the deepening of his or her faith, and to the reform of the Church. In the light of these goals, it is amazing how clearly he then saw the irreplaceable role of the laity. Wherever he went, he tried to create groups of convinced Christians who would then act as apostles in their own areas and wherever they had influence. For him, the laity was anything but a temporary resource or emergency help for priests.

Shortly after Hofbauer had arrived in Warsaw in 1787, he began to gather laypeople around him and to train them for the apostolate. As early as 1788, he formed a community of laypeople.

He called the members "Oblates" (those devoted to God). In fact, priests were accepted into this organization, but preferably it was made up of "single lay men and women." Hofbauer spells out his intentions in the introduction to the Statutes of the Oblates: "It is necessary that these people who still have the good fortune to be believers gather together in order to work with unified force against the powerful river of immorality and faithlessness."

He needed apostolically minded laypeople, that is, people who lived in families and in the world, who followed the savior there and worked as missionaries.

Lay Missionaries

Becoming holy—being an apostle and open to Christ—yet being open to humankind! Hofbauer placed his Oblates in this dialectical tension. Let us briefly list his main concerns: to follow Jesus Christ with all possible strength, to accept belief in Christ, to listen to the Word of God and to take part in the sacramental life of the Church, to be loyal to the teachings of the Church and its prayers. In no way did Hofbauer want to cultivate the sham piety of a parasite. He was concerned rather with a lay missionary spirituality. In this instance we can also summarize Hofbauer's main interests in point form: witnesses to life, family religious discussions, an apostolate of the press through the distribution of good books.

Family and Secret Society

Clement Hofbauer established very comprehensive rules for his Society of Oblates. Naturally they contain many outdated provisions which no longer correspond to our contemporary sensibilities.

The members of this society were to create a lay elite. "Since this federation is not a so-called brotherhood but rather an assembly of select individuals, only the most proven and most virtuous souls can and should be accepted into it, namely, those who are filled with the spirit of Jesus Christ and hunger for justice." Thus only those applicants may be accepted who are "leading a pious way of life and who possess a zeal for the glory of God and the salvation of souls."

The probation period lasts one year. Then the applicant may take the vows of the Oblate and receive an official certificate. The members within a country or province meet regularly. At this time, the superior gives lectures or conferences. Their meetings also take place in private homes. An important aspect of these gatherings is the exchange of ideas and experiences and an evaluation of their methods: "At these meetings, each member who has something to contribute to the specific or general propagation of good should explain the means, manner, and methods he has used to achieve it. Thus in the future one will be able to act in the same way with similar persons and under similar circumstances. At these gatherings, the members should discuss which books would be better and more useful for certain people and circumstances." This sharing of personal experiences, these small group discussions, and these analytical forums seem quite modern!

The Oblates formed something akin to a federation of friendship, much like a family. Each member tried to carry the burden of the others. Should one member die, all the others were informed. To outsiders, however, the organization of Hofbauer-followers appeared to be some kind of secret society. "This organization must remain entirely secret to nonmembers." It was supposed to work like yeast, imbuing society with the spirit of Christ from within and in silence.

Approval by the Church

This lay society spread out and prospered wherever the Redemptorists went: Poland, Germany, Austria, and in Switzerland as far as Valois. After nearly twenty years of testing, Clement Hofbauer presented the statutes for the Oblates to the Holy Father for approval. On July 29, 1804, Pope Pius VII sanctioned this lay society and its statutes. With the help of the laity and lay groups, Hofbauer certainly became a reformer of the Church.

CHAPTER 13

A Better Doer Than Leader?

F rom 1787 until 1795, Clement Maria Hofbauer rarely if ever left the city of Warsaw. During these years, he was superior of the Order at St. Benno. In addition, Father General named him his vicar on May 31, 1788. Until his death, Hofbauer would lead the branch of Redemptorists north of the Alps as the general's deputy. Since communication channels to the leadership in Italy were almost completely cut off, the vicar general had almost unlimited decision-making powers, as well as the care for the survival of the young community, which rested mainly on Clement.

Hofbauer's Goodness

Whoever wants to be a superior needs his head examined. It is by no means a picnic. Clement Hofbauer had to learn this, too. On the whole, he was not a so-called "born superior." Even his great friend Cardinal Litta conceded, "He is perhaps better suited to doing than to leading."

There is absolutely no doubt that the saint loved his confreres like a father. He was kind to them. On the other hand, he had a lively character and a hot temperament—his well-known "Hofbauer passion." One day, Brother Emmanuel Kunzmann, his former pilgrimage and hermitage companion, put him in an embarrassing situation. Emmanuel left St. Benno on his own and fled to the superior general in Rome. What had happened? We do not know, but we can assume some things. The superior general wrote his vicar in an admonishing tone: "A Superior must be, above all, good, kind, and wise. Otherwise he becomes intolerable to his subjects. Try to control your passion. Treat your subordinates with kindness and do not shock them with too much severity." The whole affair must not have been too bad; otherwise Brother Emmanuel Kunzmann would not have voluntarily returned to Hofbauer's community in Warsaw.

No Time to Be a Saint

Clement Hofbauer knew nothing of the radical separation between religious life in the monastery and the life of missionary service. He was a missionary through and through. Clement expressed himself in a letter as follows: "We unite our active life with one of contemplation. We strive to fill our external lives with fire and spirit. Without the oil of the Holy Spirit the wagon wheels of the apostolic workers squeak." Hofbauer allowed a great deal of inner freedom in the structure of community life. The Bennonites had and kept a rigid daily order, but it was in harmony with their missionary activities. Also, the Bennonites did not shut themselves off to live like monks in an enclosed monastery.

Not all the confreres were in agreement with the vicar general's ideas.[1] That is understandable. Living together in a small space with so many young people must have been a burden to many. How could it be otherwise? Thus it transpired that secret letters of complaint against the vicar general were sent to Rome to the effect that at St. Benno the Redemptorists had too many active missionary tasks and mountains of pastoral work; the silent and peaceful life of a monastery was impossible there; the prescribed rules of the Order were hardly observed; prayer was given short shrift; St. Benno was anything but a monastery.

Father Blasucci, the superior general of the Redemptorists, reacted in his own fashion. He sent a long letter to the community in Warsaw. He described how the Redemptorists lived and prayed in their monasteries in Italy. The Italian houses were cited as models for the Bennonites. This was naturally supposed to be an invitation to correct the "abuses" there.

Vicar General Hofbauer responded masterfully. For his part, he described to the superior general how one lived and worked at St. Benno. The daily order of the community in Warsaw showed, however, that one strove for a healthy balance between a life of prayer and work. If the Bennonites deviated from the customs of the Italian houses in certain things, then it was "only due to the requirements of the place, time and conditions." They were surely not disloyal because they adapted to the concrete situation there. In the north it was impossible to follow the normal daily order of the southern countries: "There is no sleeping here during the day, not even for half an hour. The climate and the people of the north were the reason. It would awake great amazement among everyone if one dared to introduce the custom of the siesta in these areas. It would be a great scandal, the community would be a laughing stock, would be considered lazy and would lose respect."

Shortly after this, Hofbauer again clarified his concerns in a second letter. Whereupon the general responded that he was really happy. He had come to the realization that the Redemptorists in Warsaw had not changed the rules and customs of the Order according to their own fancy. He understood that one had to adapt to the local situation.[2]

CHAPTER 14

St. Benno in Hindsight: An Interpretation

When we observe the life and work of Saint Clement during his time in Warsaw, we can only stand amazed. Hofbauer appears to us as a limited man. Yet, without any lengthy preparations, he became a superior of the Congregation and vicar general of the Redemptorists. Obviously, he had to learn a few things and at some cost to himself.

He always worked loyally together with the leadership in Rome. Political troubles had always rendered a lively contact between the north and the south impossible. But never once did Hofbauer think of separating himself from the original Congregation in Italy. Quite the contrary. This is indisputably a great achievement of our saint. In his dealings with the leadership, he was always open, sometimes even somewhat crude. He was a stranger to flattery. He constantly reproached the superior general that he was not interested enough in his northern confreres. Then again, he could write something quite pointed and venomous: "But, please, immediately—and not according to the usual Italian definition of immediately." "Please write so that at least I can understand it." This open, honest manner is refreshing!

Already at St. Benno, his first field of work, Father Hofbauer showed his fortunate sense for the pastoral needs of the time and the concrete conditions present there. He did not find the main springs of his initiatives in the government's legal decrees or even

in the rules of his own Congregation. This full-blooded missionary started rather with the concrete realities of life. In the emer-
gencies of the time, he saw a call from God. For him, events were
an expression of the divine will.

Hofbauer remained remarkably flexible in his apostolic methods. With a missionary's sensitivity, he tried new ways to realize
the Redemptorists' ideal. For him, it is not this or that form of
activity that is important, but rather that "the Gospel be preached
to the poor anew." The vicar general was stubbornly tenacious in
the pursuit of his missionary goals; in his pastoral methods, on
the other hand, he could adapt to the situation masterfully.

The Bennonites did not simply do everything in Warsaw. They
chose those activities that corresponded best to the ideal and charisma of their Congregation and which could best be achieved in
Warsaw. The Rules of the Order in Warsaw of 1798, which they
had on hand at the time, contained two main tasks for the Congregation: on the one hand, the preaching of the Gospel through
sermons, catechetical teachings, and spiritual exercises; on the
other, the formation of the young and the education of poor and
abandoned children.

In regard to the pastoral work at St. Benno, three main things
occur to us:

First, Hofbauer strove with his broad vision not only for the
salvation of the individual's soul, but he was also concerned with
the well-being of the entire person. He regarded education as a
missionary service with broad and long-term effects. Christian education is catechism. In teaching young people, one is instructing
the fathers and the mothers of tomorrow. Hofbauer said that the
work of the Bennonites was essentially a service for the state and
society.

Second, he blazed new ground in that he took laypeople and
their honest work for the sake of the Church seriously. Hofbauer
and his confreres systematically formed laypeople for an active
role. He called them to collaboration, and bound them together
in communities: the Society of Oblates; widows were invited to be
teachers; even a community of nuns he had envisioned to teach
and care for the sick.

Third, Clement believed in the international character and the union of all people. Hofbauer was a man with a catholic heart who felt and lived with the whole world. His homeland was a border country where blood was mixed and peoples of different nations encountered one another. The international character of Hofbauer was present from the beginning when his Czech father Dvořak married his German mother Steer and gave him life.

In Polish Warsaw at the time, there also lived a good many Germans, Russians, and Frenchmen. Various languages and mentalities collided. St. Benno constituted something like a unifying shrine for the nations. The school at St. Benno was open to all who were poor: Poles and Germans and Russians, Catholics and others. In the church of St. Benno each one could hear the Good News of the Gospel in his own language.

Hofbauer—who had often crossed the border from Moravia to Italy, from Austria to Poland—will once again move from one country to another: to Switzerland, to Germany and to France. He will dream of Russia, America, England, and Canada. He will be at home everywhere and yet not have a permanent home of his own. This man, who had his limits, carried within himself a limitless heart.

Part Three

Clement Is Hunted
Everywhere
1795–1808

CHAPTER 15

A Saint Dreams

C lement Maria Hofbauer was someone greatly seized by Christ. "The love of Christ urges us on" (2 Corinthians 5:14). Clement saw the suffering of so many people. He saw the great harvest and the small number of workers.

For thirty years, Hofbauer dreamed of an international seminary for the training of missionaries. This plan became his favorite idea, almost an obsession. He wrote, "With the greatest impatience, I want to offer myself completely to our Savior and to those souls who have been saved by his blood....I need a solid foundation where I can gather co-workers and train them in their duties....I strongly hope that we will have a great host of missionaries there with which we may come to the aid of all the Church's needs everywhere in the world. I would gather Frenchmen, Germans, Poles, and people of other nations in order to send them by twos into those countries to which God will call them."

Clement was not an idle dreamer. His plans were daring and almost global in scope. In fact, Clement seemed to want to go everywhere. The superior general believed he had to rein in this insatiable desire: "I must point out that you must learn to moderate your all too fiery zeal to establish houses of our Congregation in every nation." Hofbauer's answer shows his sense of the Church's missionary purpose. His first concern was not to expand the Congregation. He was led rather by the concern for the increase of the glory of God: "As far as human frailty will allow, I want to work for the salvation of souls through new foundations." And, in fact, his attempts to found new houses are quite numerous.[1]

It was, however, to be the fate of our saint that his heartfelt dreams for an international seminary for missionaries could never be realized and that the planned foundations either died in the planning stages or did not last long.

In the Pincers of an Antireligious Government

When the Polish kingdom was erased from the world map in 1795–1796, the Bennonites found themselves in an unpleasant position. The antireligious government of Prussia put St. Benno into a vise.

On the one hand, the southern Prussian officials ridiculed the life of the Order of the Bennonites. They sneered ironically and sarcastically that whoever wanted to be a monk at St. Benno had only to bring a completely empty head with him. Moreover, he had to be prepared to waste his time in mechanical, useless preoccupations. St. Benno produced only dreamers or hypocrites. The strict discipline of the monastery supported despotism in the hierarchy. The sneering went on and on.

The government also undertook legal actions that would lead inevitably to the death of every religious community. The state claimed the right to regulate and supervise novitiate life; lay brothers were no longer allowed to be accepted; the candidates for the priesthood were only allowed to join the Order at the age of twenty-four and only with the written permission of the government; all communications with the superiors of the Congregation outside the country were strictly forbidden; each Bennonite had to decide whether he wanted to act as a teacher or a pastor. In black and white, this meant that whoever undertook teaching duties was no longer allowed to fulfill any missionary functions. The insidious intent of such forced servitude is quite clear: the monasteries were supposed to disappear gradually. An official memo reads: "A plan which naturally must remain secret."

Father Hofbauer saw it all clearly: "The godless officials do everything in order to starve the monasteries and to exterminate the members of the Orders." The vicar general of the Redemptorists saw only one way to save his community from extinction in this desperate situation. He had to find a solid foundation in another country. And so Hofbauer made the daring step across the border.

St. Benno in Warsaw.

CHAPTER 16

Trips to Establish
New Foundations

T he Redemptorists undertook missionary activity in Courland (Lettland) southwest of Riga in 1795. The foundation at Mitau awakened great hopes in Clement Hofbauer. Unfortunately, this establishment suffered a terrible end after a very short time. This failure was a bitter disappointment for Hofbauer.[1] Other very promising plans also burst like soap bubbles.

Hofbauer's First Trip to Establish a New Foundation: August to December 1795

The papal nuncio in Lucerne had approached Hofbauer regarding the establishment of a foundation in the diocese of Constance. On August 30, 1795, Hofbauer and Hübl left Warsaw. They traveled through Prague, Ratisbon, Augsburg, and Lindau to Constance. But they had to turn back because of unforeseen events. The war in southern Germany left them no other choice. On the journey home through Vienna, Clement wanted to make a quick visit to his home village of Tasswitz. When Hofbauer and Hübl arrived there, both Redemptorists were bombarded with a thousand and one questions. Clement told of his school in Warsaw. Several fathers asked him to accept their sons into the school at St. Benno. Thus Hofbauer took four boys from his home village back to Warsaw with him. They arrived at St. Benno in the first half of December.

Clement could not know that in the meantime all hell had broken loose in Tasswitz. The police combed the countryside looking for the hardened criminal Clement Hofbauer. He had violated the so-called Emigration Act of 1784. There were embarrassingly detailed investigations in Tasswitz, endless interrogations of Hofbauer's relatives, and long police reports. This completely harmless event was played up into a criminal "child-kidnapping." Dire consequences were to follow.

Second Trip to Establish a Foundation in Wollerau: July 1797 to August 1798

A delegation from Switzerland arrived in Warsaw in May 1796. These representatives fervently asked Hofbauer to establish a Latin school and an orphanage—fashioned along the lines of the one at St. Benno—in the Canton of Switz.

On July 11, 1797, Hofbauer left Warsaw with his companions.[2] Their journey took them through Vienna, Munich, and Constance. The four Redemptorists arrived in Wollerau on Lake Zurich in the middle of September. Clement and his companions moved into a house occupied by the Penitent Brothers.[3]

We are poorly informed about the details of Hofbauer's stay in the Canton of Switz. A few things are clear, however, from the many police reports. A small beginning was made with the schools in Wollerau. From Wollerau, Clement undertook various trips into Switzerland and beyond. Due to general inflation and the lack of funds, the small community soon ran into great difficulty. In addition, French troops threatened invasion at any moment. Hofbauer's continued presence in Switzerland became impossible.

There were also other misfortunes that we know next to nothing about that made Clement's stay in Wollerau a martyrdom.[4] His health had deteriorated badly, and on top of this suffering, no letters from his colleagues at St. Benno had gotten through to Switzerland. These difficulties all added up. Even saints are only human. What had to happen, happened. Hofbauer suffered a mental breakdown and fell into a deep depression.

Wollerau in Switzerland. Hofbauer and his colleagues lived in this house from September 1797 to February 1798.

Misperceptions

When a letter from Warsaw finally did arrive in Wollerau, matters came to a head. The letter from the Bennonites stated that there would hopefully soon be a new, solid foundation in Switzerland. Vicar General Hofbauer reacted improperly, as a sick man would. He misinterpreted this well-meaning remark to mean that they were happy at St. Benno to be finally rid of Clement. The saint must have answered in an uncommonly irritated manner in his letter of December 6.

Clement's colleagues in Warsaw were shocked when they received Hofbauer's letter. Greatly grieved, Hübl wrote his friend, "My God, how can you imagine that I or anyone else here would not be glad to see you come back? Would such terrible behavior be compatible with the gratitude and love that I and all of us owe you and feel for you?...My heart bleeds whenever I think of your position; but at present we ourselves have but seven ducats to our name."

On the same day (January 20), Jestershein also wrote to Hofbauer: "Just come home, everyone is expecting you with joy and our children will rush to you with open arms....Dearest Father, one thing more, but do not take it the wrong way. I must complain against this mistrust....No, dearest Father! I do not have such a nasty heart, not such a black soul, that would repay such mildness with ingratitude, but rather a heart which loves you."

Father Jestershein found just the right words for his letter to the other colleagues in Wollerau: "How often your young stomachs must have growled for Polish bread. We would be glad to learn whether you are out of that worrisome wood yet."

Into Prison

Hofbauer, his colleague Kopsch, and the leader of the Penitent Brothers left the "nagging hole" of Wollerau on February 14, 1798. They traveled over Garmisch-Partenkirchen to Augsburg. The others were supposed to follow in a few weeks.

They met up in mid March at Wiesent. The journey continued on foot, by boat, and on a farmer's cart. On April 21, they arrived at five in the evening in Cracow and underwent a passport check. At the checkpoint, the police identified Clement as a wanted man from Tasswitz, as a kidnapper of children. Hofbauer was immediately arrested, taken away, and placed under house arrest at the Dominican monastery. A suspenseful novel of accusations begins. The police conduct painfully exact interrogations, and the investigative forces of half the empire are set in motion. Files are sent back and forth—as is the case when dealing with internationally wanted, hardened criminals. The judgment of the officials was quite clear: "The apprehended religious must be viewed as a true adventurer due to his indeterminate travels within the empire and abroad." And this conclusion was not entirely misplaced!

A True Adventurer

Days pass. The chicanery of the police continues. Finally, after seven weeks, a decision arrives, a terrible ultimatum: either the "kidnapped" young people who left Tasswitz with their parents' permission are delivered to the authorities in Moravia—or the prisoner remains in jail for life. What to do? Hofbauer has the four boys brought to Cracow. From there, they are taken to their homes in Tasswitz. Now Clement hopes to be in Warsaw by mid July at the latest.

But—another bomb goes off. The police discovered another

hot lead. Two other Austrians are still at St. Benno. The proce-
dure begins all over again: interrogations, negotiations, reports—
and new interrogations and new reports. Enough is enough! Clement is at the end of his rope! He curses the Austrian government
and uses "most inappropriate language," as one police report
states. Clement's arrest already lasted 106 days. Rebellion is boil-
ing within Hofbauer; on the afternoon of August 5, he puts an
end to this situation. He flees and succeeds in getting across the
border. On the morning of August 6, the police come to get Clement for further interrogations. But—the cell is empty: "The bird
has flown."

Hofbauer was in Warsaw again by mid August. He arrived
there completely exhausted. So, his second trip to establish a new
foundation ended quite miserably. Humanly speaking, it had
brought him only ordeals, suffering, illness, and bitterness.

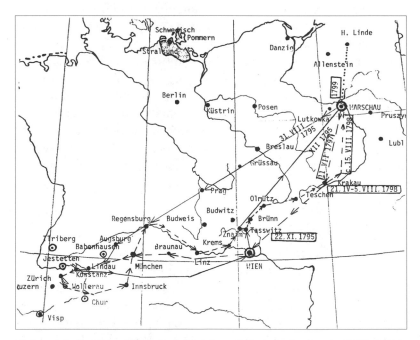

Hofbauer's first three trips to establish foundations took place in 1795, 1797–
98, and 1799.

The Third Trip to Establish a Foundation: 1799

In the following year, Hofbauer accepted an invitation from what was then East Prussian Ermland. Once again he took on the difficulties of the trip. The conditions for a mission-station, especially at the shrine of Lindau were very favorable. But this trip was destined to failure because Hofbauer did not have the necessary people.

CHAPTER 17

Good Friday on
Mount Tabor—Jestetten
1802–1806

T he French revolutionary troops were burning and ravaging their way across Europe. The Enlightenment, Rationalism, and an "Anti-Rome Complex" were building a common front even within the Catholic Church.

Hofbauer and the Bennonites were living more and more dangerously in Warsaw. The government of southern Prussia did everything to force them out of the country. If Clement wanted to assure the continued existence of his community, the vicar general definitely had to have a second foundation somewhere.

A new foundation seemed to be in the offing in southern Germany in 1802. During his stay in Switzerland, Hofbauer may have met the priest Heinrich Rigolet.[1] Perhaps they even went together to Jestetten near Schaffhausen. There on the top of what is called Mount Tabor were the remains of a fortress. The ruined castle was now a convent. The community of sisters was heavily indebted, however; and in the meantime, it had shrunk to a mere two members.

After lengthy negotiations, the time had come. On November 11, 1802, Hofbauer left the city of Warsaw with three confreres.[2] God's gypsies arrived in Constance on December 27. Hofbauer immediately presented himself to the bishop's vicar general, Ignatius, Baron von Wessenberg. There, for the first time, these two important men of the church met.

Wessenberg and Hofbauer were typical representatives of two opposing streams within the Church reform movement.[3] Their plans for renewal were fundamentally different. These differences and their opposition did not surface during their first encounter. On the contrary, each made a great impression on the other. Hofbauer even received from Wessenberg all the necessary permissions for pastoral ministry. Then the four Redemptorists continued their journey in good spirits and arrived in Jestetten on December 30.

Terrible Awakening on Mount Tabor

Father Hofbauer was shocked when they arrived on Mount Tabor. The weather had inflicted substantial damage to the castle buildings. Hofbauer wrote from Jestetten while still under the shock of this first sight: "If I want to be honest, I must admit that I am terribly shocked....When I saw the condition of this house, I almost lost courage....Had I known everything, it would have been rash to come here."

But giving up at the first sign of difficulty was not Clement's way. As early as the second day, Hofbauer preached three times in the castle church. On Mount Tabor he immediately began the perpetual mission modeled on the format of St. Benno's in Warsaw. The people were enthusiastic and streamed to Jestetten from everywhere. Within a few weeks, ten young men presented themselves for admission into the Redemptorist Congregation. There was no shortage of candidates, but rather one of space and money: "What am I to do? Where shall I put them? How shall I feed them?" If only he had a house of studies![4]

The Family at Mount Tabor Grows

Vicar General Hofbauer called Father Passerat from Warsaw to Jestetten and named him superior of the new community. The new rector arrived in Jestetten on July 2, 1803. In the fall of 1804, the community at Jestetten numbered six priests, four brothers, nine novices, and several students. But the living conditions were inhuman: "A single large room served as refectory and study hall and, along with two other rooms, comprised the entire monastery. The students, the novices, and also some the priests have their bedrooms in the attic of the chapel, and I live in the summer with some others in an old tower in the garden where one must protect oneself against the rain and weather with boards rather than glass in the windows. The door cannot be closed; and one climbs up on a rickety ladder." This description of conditions is reported by trustworthy witnesses.

They earned their living themselves. Hofbauer often went with his colleagues into the fields to work. As soon as the vicar general had some cash, he spent it in order to lower the enormous debts of the nuns and to calm the many creditors.

The Devil's General

The Duke and the faithful were full of praise for the moral behavior and the missionary zeal of the priests. Yet threatening storm clouds were brewing over Mount Tabor.

The pastor of Jestetten was filled with the spirit of the Enlightenment. He very quickly revealed himself to be a sworn enemy of the Redemptorists. His behavior grew increasingly bolder until he finally forbade his parishioners to attend the sermons or go to confession at Mount Tabor. He threatened to withhold Easter Communion from anyone who did not respect this edict.

The prefect of Jestetten, named Teufel (which means "devil" in German), also raged against the Redemptorists: "I cannot hide my aversion for this new Hofbauer Institute." In hate-filled, incendiary tirades, he called Hofbauer a "dangerous, crawling snake that has slid into the German Fatherland behind a mask of piety." Absurd rumors were spread about Hofbauer, among which that "with brooms and jugs, with cow bells and ropes on their necks," he forced "the women to go to holy Communion."

To stay in Jestetten any longer was impossible under such conditions. The Redemptorists left Mount Tabor in November 1805. Once again, Hofbauer knew deep disappointment, and this time one with a bitter aftertaste.

Mount Tabor in Jestetten (Baden): December 1802 until November 1805. At the time, part of the Redemptorist Community lived in this tower.

Bitter Aftertaste

In 1806, the women's convent, whose debts were enormously high, was dissolved. Everything was supposed to be sold. The creditors were called in to make their claims. So Hofbauer also presented the bill for the monies owed to the monastery and for his other possessions. The former superioress of the house, Ida Kasparin, was now harried by the prefect, Teufel, and his sympathizers. Whereupon Kasparin presented Hofbauer with an inflated counter bill. With a bitter heart, Hofbauer was forced to defend himself. Hofbauer's six-page justification is a thorough settling of accounts with the former superioress. The language of this letter could not be clearer. Each sentence betrays Hofbauer's inner tension and also something of the ferocity of his character: "Whenever I and my brothers had nothing else on the table but potatoes with salt, cooked in water, the ladies treated themselves well in their refectory under the pretext that they were ill....We have served the ladies more than they have served us. We fed them, dried their tears of hunger with our sweat, and with my money brought them out of debt....Such a process is worse than that of a street thief because one can defend oneself against him, but not against a person who acts this way."

Clement was represented in court by the former civil servant Brenzinger. The trial dragged on and lasted until the summer of 1808. Then there was a compromise. Each party renounced any further claims; the court costs were divided.

Hofbauer memorial stone at Altersheim in Jestetten.

CHAPTER 18

The Fanatics in Triberg
1805–1807

While Clement Maria Hofbauer was active in Jestetten, his reputation spread quickly throughout the area. So it happened that one day a delegation from the citizens of Triberg arrived in Jestetten. They sought Hofbauer to take over the missions at the Shrine of Mary in the Pines.

At the time, Triberg, in the Black Forest, was a small village. There were one hundred and fifty-one families and eight hundred inhabitants who lived mainly from the shrine and its pilgrims. Some days, several thousand pilgrims arrived there. The emissaries from Triberg explained that the shrine was presently being neglected, that there was a shortage of suitable confessors, and that many other things were in a bad way. They begged and pleaded for Hofbauer to help them.

At the beginning of July 1803, Hofbauer and Passerat sneaked across the French border dressed as workers and made their way to Joinville, where Passerat's mother lived. They returned to Jestetten safely. As early as July 13, Hofbauer and Hübl marched to Triberg in order to inspect the place. The enthusiastic pilgrim in Hofbauer began to dream: this pastorate could become something like a perpetual mission; the house near the church could house about thirty-five people and was well suited to be a novitiate and a house of studies.

The vicar general gave the citizens of Triberg a provisional

decision. First, the Tribergers would have to get the permission of
the local government and of the diocese. Then the Redemptorists
would be able to take over the pastoral work of the shrine, perhaps in 1804. Shortly thereafter, on August 24, Clement began
his last trip to Rome. Its high point must have been the audience
with Pope Pius VII. Hofbauer would again be traveling for more
than a year.[1]

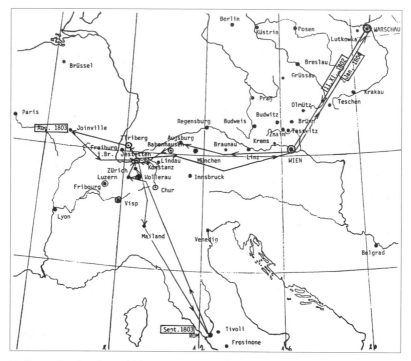

Hofbauer's trips from 1802 to 1804.

Tug of War Around a Pilgrimage

In the meantime, some very tough negotiations were under way.
Letters were sent back and forth. Pressure and demands came
from one side, delaying tactics and refusals came from the other.
Wessenberg, the bishop's representative and a passionate opponent of pilgrimages, defended himself to the maximum. Finally,
the parties agreed on a compromise. Wessenberg set two condi-

tions: only three priests were permitted to work for the pilgrims at the shrine, and their tenure was limited to six months. That agreement was reached in mid May 1805.

Between Veneration and Contempt

Hofbauer immediately left Jestetten for Triberg with five priests and eleven high-school students. The trip was made on foot and in driving rain. Tired, they arrived at a farmhouse. The missionaries had to spend the night on straw in a barn. When the people of Triberg heard that the priests were on the way, a real frenzy of joy broke out. At the end of May, the people received the Redemptorists in triumph and accompanied them to the shrine. This shrine could hold only some of the pilgrims. Father Hofbauer climbed into the pulpit for the first time. His sermon made an unbelievably deep impression.

Hofbauer stayed in Triberg for only about ten weeks, until mid August 1805. In this short time, there was an unexpected increase in the number of pilgrimages. The people simply called him "the saint." Pilgrims arrived in droves from everywhere. From early morning until late at night, the confessionals were besieged by long lines.

But soon, misfortune again descended mercilessly upon this new foundation. In July, Hofbauer had three of his theology students ordained priests by the papal nuncio in Lucerne. When Wessenberg learned of these ordinations, he was greatly angered. His good will toward Hofbauer turned into implacable opposition. There was a complete break with the Redemptorists. Wessenberg let himself get carried away. He called Hofbauer's followers "notorious idiots, bigots and dreamers." At the beginning of August, he lashed out against Hofbauer. He put all his powers into play. Hofbauer tried to change Wessenberg's mind. The saint explained to him in a moving letter what had actually happened; if he should have been amiss, he asked for forgiveness. This request for forgiveness was made in vain. Wessenberg would not be placated. The priests would have to leave Triberg after six months.

The freethinkers and opponents of the Church in the entire area banded together in order to vent their rage at "these insuffer-

The Shrine of Mary in the Pines near Triberg in the Black Forest. Hofbauer preached here in 1805.

able guests." Shivers run down one's spine when one reads the hateful and slanderous documents. Let's take a few random labels that were used against the Redemptorists: "weeds," "these parasitical people," "band of beggars," "Pharisee sect preaching ill-omens and mischief," "the superstitious Thaborite monster," "a terribly fanatical horde." "It would have been best if these Polacks had never been let into Triberg, [because] these Italian Liguorians are taking bread away from our own poor."

The government and the chief bailiff of Triberg, on the contrary, again and again praised these model priests, who, due to their unpretentiousness and their zeal for souls, "stood in high regard with the entire people." And, in fact, the whole population of Triberg was almost entirely on the side of the Redemptorists. It is touching to see with how much love the faithful were attached to these "model priests." The people even declared themselves prepared to supply food and clothing for the members of the Order. When it became known that the expulsion of the Redemptorists was already decided, the anger among the population grew so great that it seemed that an uprising might be in the offing.[2]

On May 16, 1807, the last Redemptorist left the pilgrimage shrine at Triberg. Father Casimir Langanki described his frame of mind in a letter to Clement Hofbauer with these words: "Finally, I have been freed from my moral prison." The official report of the bailiff's office captured an entirely different view: "This departure was indeed peaceful but caused the deepest pain among most of the population."

CHAPTER 19

Like Hunted Game—
Babenhausen-Chur
1805–1807

In the summer of 1805, Clement Hofbauer found himself in a completely hopeless situation. He realized with great disappointment that his Congregation could no longer function in the Diocese of Constance. The complete dissolution of the foundations in Jestetten and Triberg was only a matter of time.

Hoping against all hope, the vicar general attempted a foundation in the Diocese of Augsburg. Two of his proven friends and patrons came to his aid. Clement contacted Duke Anselm M. Fugger, who possessed the tiny imperial principality of Babenhausen, south of Ulm.[1] The negotiations went off without a hitch. A house was rented. In November 1805, nearly thirty Redemptorists and candidates lived there. But the "monastery" was very unhealthy because water ran down the walls. Everything betrayed poverty. What served as the dining and study hall during the day was turned into a dormitory at night by spreading straw on the bare floor.

In Babenhausen

The priests in Babenhausen took over the pastoral work in the hospital, dedicated themselves to the teaching of the youth, and functioned as auxiliary parish priests. Hofbauer reported enthusiastically to Warsaw: "One can achieve something here! I preach on Sunday. People come from hours away when they knew that a priest from our Congregation would preach....I speak like a Swabian."

In Babenhausen, as elsewhere, the priests were incredibly esteemed by some, while they were otherwise persecuted by their rationalist opponents.

Due to a shortage of space in the accommodations at Babenhausen, Hofbauer had to walk every evening with a few others to the neighboring village of Weinried where Father Wagner was a great friend to the Redemptorists. He had offered them accommodation in his own rectory. Father Wagner's saying became a familiar quotation in the area: "Give me four Hofbauers for the pulpit and four Passerats for the confessional and I will convert entire kingdoms."

Shattered Hopes Once Again

Clement Hofbauer could breathe easier, but success would not last long. Already a new misfortune stood waiting at the door as if everything had conspired against Clement. The political troubles were coming to a dramatic head.

Anselm M. Fugger, the imperial prince of Babenhausen, was well disposed toward the Redemptorists. But in bordering Bavaria, the all-powerful government minister Maximilian Joseph Montgelas ruled. This inveterate partisan of the Enlightenment was a sworn enemy of the Church and of all monasteries. Through an alliance with France, he became Napoleon's agent. In keeping with the mentality of the French Revolution and of the Enlightenment, he brought the Church under the powerful whip of the state.

At the beginning of 1806, increasingly stubborn rumors circulated that Montgelas wanted to annex the principality of Babenhausen to Bavaria. Hofbauer did not know what to do. He clearly saw that if Babenhausen went to Bavaria, the Redemptorists would have only one thing left to do: "To flee as quickly as possible." His letter to the nuncio sounds like a cry for help: "New circumstances have destroyed beautiful hopes."

Then, Hofbauer broke down again. He became ill, seriously

Pulpit in Weinried. Hofbauer often preached here because Father Wagner was a great friend to the Redemptorists.

ill. He was no longer up to the internal and external tensions. The worst was feared. His friend Hübl even wrote to Superior General Blasucci that Clement suffered unbelievably in Germany. The superior general should determine what was to be done if Vicar General Hofbauer should die.

But Clement was tough by nature, and he recovered. Still, on August 5, the time of crisis had arrived. The principality of Babenhausen was swallowed up by Bavaria. The next day, Hofbauer wrote to St. Benno: he had lost all hope that they would be allowed to stay in Babenhausen. Clement's health was still not perfect. Since he no longer knew where to go with his people, he would begin his journey without delay in order to find shelter for the winter.

Hofbauer's statements later in this letter appear as a superhuman effort by the saint to climb out of the grave dug for his dead hopes: "Come on! Courage! God is the Lord. He guides everything to His glory and for our best. No one can resist Him. All of man's plans—no matter how well thought through—serve God in the end in order to realize His holy will. I have given myself completely to His will in this hopeless situation."

Hoping Against Hope

On the following day, he again wrote to Warsaw. What he reported to his friend Hübl was strange. After a great struggle, he had decided finally to emigrate to Canada in order to establish a foundation there: "Sometimes I lose my breath. I creep like a shadow! Before I leave this earth, I would like to find a shelter for my poor children....With what joy we study the maps! You think we are crazy, right? But what to do? Our decision is taken...." How jumpy is the train of thought in this letter! With how many emotions are his words charged! His new plan greatly excited the vicar general.

A Great Farewell

And then everything takes on a new and dramatic twist. All of a sudden, Clement decides to travel to Vienna. He wants to meet Hübl there. He takes along the theology student, Martin Stark, as a traveling companion. Clement takes his leave from his companions. Many of them he will not see again. Without knowing it, he also takes his leave of southern Germany, of Babenhausen, and of Weinried forever.

On the journey, he meets two French soldiers. One of them draws his sword and holds it against Hofbauer's chest. He imperiously demands Hofbauer's coat and then disappears.

On September 3, Clement Hofbauer and Martin Stark arrive in Vienna. Hübl also arrives there. The three Redemptorists must remain in the city on the Danube for two months. One after another, reports of war and bloodshed arrive. Hofbauer can no longer return to Babenhausen. He decides to travel to St. Benno with Hübl and Stark. They leave Vienna on November 5.

In Cracow, the borders are closed. They must make a long detour via Pruszyn. This long journey becomes one long martyrdom for Hofbauer. The winter is cruelly harsh. And Clement is terribly sick again. He cannot eat solid food. He has neither a coat nor hat, not even proper socks and shoes. Finally, the Bennonites arrive in Pruszyn on December 2, where a friend, a count-

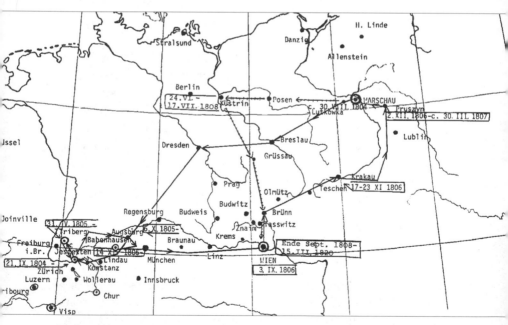

Hofbauer's journeys from 1804 to 1808.

ess, takes them into her castle. They stay there four months. Sickness, a closed border, and difficulties with their passports make continuing their journey impossible. For on November 28, the French troops under Marshal Davoust had marched into Warsaw.

More Bad News

Sad news arrives at the castle of the countess. There is great misery at St. Benno. There is a lack of funds. The army is quartered in the house. The community is disheartened. On instructions from the sick vicar general, Hübl writes a long letter of comfort and warning to colleagues in Warsaw: "Drive away your fears....Do not be discouraged. Do not doubt that the good Lord will help us."

And on February 9, Hofbauer receives even more sad news from Babenhausen that gives him sleepless nights. In September the Redemptorists were ordered to leave the territory of the Bavarian States and thus the former principality of Babenhausen. Where should they go? There is no place of refuge. One last hope remains: Switzerland. Father Passerat travels to Switzerland to find asylum there.

Finally, a new glimmer of hope arises. In November the priests are offered a place of refuge in the Premonstratensian monastery of St. Lucius in Chur. By December the negotiations are going at top speed. In January 1807, the Redemptorists are forbidden to do any pastoral work in Babenhausen. In small groups, the priests head for Chur. Father Rector Passerat leaves Babenhausen on January 5, in biting cold, he wades to Chur through deep snow. Now there are ten Redemptorists in Chur and eleven still in Babenhausen. But these eleven must soon take flight.[2]

In Warsaw

Hofbauer received all of these bad news during his forced stay in the castle of Pruszyn. His heart was bleeding because even his last foundation in southern Germany had ended so pitifully. The political conditions and the spirit of the Enlightenment were stronger than his plans, but not stronger than his faith. Finally, Hofbauer was able to leave the countess' castle and return home to Warsaw. At the end of March, he arrived at St. Benno, a man broken in health. After a separation of two and a half years, he could see and embrace his afflicted colleagues once again.

CHAPTER 20

Death Takes Its Toll
June–July 1807

C lement Hofbauer had been back at St. Benno for some
time now. He regained his health slowly. In the meantime, the political situation had also calmed down a bit.
The Bennonites were allowed to work unhindered after the French
troops marched into Warsaw. Even the confreres in Switzerland
reported good news from Chur. Thus the sun shone again on the
vicar general. The saint could hardly have imagined that the most
difficult year in his life (June 1807 to June 1808) was about to begin.

Clement Hofbauer had a deep sense of family. He loved his
religious family and the founder of the Congregation, Alphonsus
Liguori. The death of a colleague very much hurt this man who
had a rough shell but a soft heart. When four confreres died within
three days during the summer of 1796, he wrote: "Our community has suffered a terrible loss. God's will be done. But the pain
almost crushes us."

Around the middle of 1807, one of the heaviest misfortunes
hit him. Clement would not recover from this blow for a long
time.

Beloved Father Hübl

Father Thaddeus Hübl was Hofbauer's most intimate friend, and
enjoyed Clement's complete trust. Hübl was considered a very

lovable person; he possessed an extraordinary knowledge and enjoyed the greatest respect in Warsaw. For this reason especially, this excellent priest was particularly hated by the enemies of the Church. Terrible things happened as a result of this hatred.

One night, Hübl was called to a dying man. Picked up by a carriage, he climbed into it, but suddenly someone gagged and blindfolded him. The carriage took off at a breakneck speed. Finally, the carriage stopped in front of a hut. The priest was dragged into a dark room. Instead of a sick man, some men were waiting for the hated Bennonite. The ruffians attacked and beat him. Hübl was supposed to promise never again to hear the confessions of certain women. The priest refused to promise. The ruffians attacked him again. They tore off his clothes and beat him with clubs.

Badly beaten and tied up, Hübl was returned to St. Benno. He would recover from this merciless attack very slowly. As soon as this tireless missionary was feeling a little better, he went to the military hospital to visit the soldiers sick with typhus. Through his pastoral service, Hübl himself was infected with the deadly disease. The fever increased. He grew worse from day to day. The doctors were powerless. Hofbauer spent almost day and night at his friend's deathbed. Hübl passed away in Hofbauer's arms on July 4.

What must Clement have felt as he held the dead body of his best friend in his arms! Surely the touching story of their friendship of more than twenty years must have passed before his eyes one more time: their student days in Vienna, their evening discussions in the Christian Friendship circle around Diessbach, their pilgrimage to Rome, entering the Congregation, the day they were ordained priests, their adventurous journey north, their close cooperation in building St. Benno, their monthlong journeys to southern Germany and to Italy. Hübl had been his right-hand advisor, Clement's inseparable, lifelong companion. And now this good man lies there—dead—dead in the prime of his life, only forty-seven years old.

Deep Wounds

Hofbauer was completely devastated. He lost his composure and his grip. Even saints have hearts that bleed. Clement's wounded heart bled, and the wound did not want to heal.

Three months after Hübl's death, Clement wrote: "The wound is deep. It hurts. It is difficult to bear." Hofbauer lamented his loss again in a letter a month and a half later: "The death of my first companion to the north, Father Hübl, destroyed my composure.... During meditation at the feet of the crucified Savior, one seems prepared for everything. But as soon as the Lord wants to place His cross upon us, one is too clumsy to carry it. I am just such a donkey." Clement also wrote, "In the hour of testing one forgets all the good plans. This happened to me at the death of my brother." Four and one-half months after the death of his friend, Clement was still saddened: "I am convinced that our Father Hübl is already in heaven and rejoices with Christ. But having said that, I cannot conquer the great pain that weighs upon me. I surrender to the will of God. I swear always to want only what God wants and yet I must admit that since Hübl's death I have not had a single happy hour." Only at the beginning of the following year could Clement report that he had recovered from the shock: "I have calmed down somewhat since the death of Father Hübl, but I am still filled with sadness."

Only he who has loved deeply can suffer so much. Such friendships and such an ability to feel suffering make the saints more accessible to us. Hofbauer's lament at the death of his friend reminds me of the great friendship which once bound David and Jonathan. After the death of his friend, David sang: "I grieve for you, my brother Jonathan; how dear you were to me! How wonderful was your love for me, better even than the love of women. The brave soldier has fallen" (2 Samuel 1:26).

Consolation of the Saints

The typhus epidemic in Warsaw did not just tear the most beloved person from the side of the vicar general. The insidious disease also took away Father Passerat's countryman and companion, Father Vannelet. Thus the rector at Chur lost the last of his French friends who had entered the Congregation with him. Passerat experienced some bitter hours in faraway Grisons. He, too, was shattered and almost paralyzed with pain. The superior of the refugee group in Chur had still other worries, as we shall soon see. He wrote to his superior Hofbauer in a depressed mood that he would prefer it be he, if only death would save him. Although Clement almost broke under his own sadness, he would not accept such talk. His response to Passerat is a master stroke of Christian spirituality: "We must obediently pray to Divine Providence. We must kiss the hand that strikes us a hundred times. For it can heal our wounds. The departed have gone to their glory. And you want to die? Out of love for Christ? Or out of love for "the flesh"—in order to escape the cross? To suffer and to hang on the cross with Christ is better than dying."

CHAPTER 21

Flight From Chur to Visp November 1807

The misfortunes of the times persecuted Clement and his community at every turn. It is hard to believe, but the next disaster was already on its way. This time it hit the community in Grisons. The foundation at Chur was only provisional and in danger from the very beginning. Father Rector Passerat left for the Valais in May 1807. He wanted to look for a sanctuary for his community there in the event of an expulsion at short notice from Chur. And Passerat was lucky. The pastor of Visp, Adrian de Courten, the council of state of the Republic of Valais and the bishop of Sitten offered asylum to the Redemptorists.

In the meantime, the issue of the Redemptorists in Chur had already caused a downright religious feud. The antireligious government of Bavaria made its influence felt and asked the government of Grisons to keep the Redemptorists away from the Bavarian border since they were enemies of the state. On October 25, 1807, the Bavarian ambassador, Johann von Orly, demanded that the magistrate of Switzerland finally ensure that the Liguorians be expelled from Chur: "The time has come to put an end to this nonsense that is the ruination of states and a misuse of religiosity. The hidden snake lurks in ambush, stores up poison, breeds treason and sharpens its deadly tooth, perhaps even on the breast of the hospitable benefactor....Thus in the interest of the common good and according to the state's political wisdom, the removal of these dangerous monks is desired by the government of Switzerland and that of Bavaria."

This demand, couched in strange diplomatic language from a powerful neighbor, did not miss its mark. As early as November, the Redemptorists were forced to leave Chur. Once more, Father Rector Passerat called his monastic community together. He told his confreres: "Do not be afraid, my brothers. It is indeed hard to flee in the middle of winter; but Divine Providence has certainly already prepared another place for us."

Then touching scenes took place. Four youths, all under sixteen, also lived in the community. All four later wished to enter the Congregation of the Redemptorists. Father Rector Passerat was of the opinion that it would be irresponsible to take these young boys with them on their flight in the middle of winter. Thus he told them directly that they had to return to their parents. One of this group of four would later report: "When we heard this we began to cry and sob loudly. We went into the chapel and threw ourselves onto the floor before the altar of the Mother of God. With outstretched arms we prayed aloud. Some time later, Father Passerat entered the chapel. As soon as he heard us praying, he was moved emotionally. He allowed us to come with him to Valais."

The Apostles Are Coming

In order to attract as little attention as possible, the community divided itself into four groups. They were supposed to march to Visp independently of one another by different routes. They found themselves on the road once again. One of these gypsies of God described the travel habits of the Liguorians roughly as follows: "We undertook our journeys almost exclusively on foot, and that in every kind of weather. We had stowed our possessions in our knapsacks: clothing, books, and the most necessary items. Usually we covered about ten miles a day. We always wore the habit of our Order. These were so worn that we resembled a troop of beggars. Wherever we arrived, the curious stared at us. Sometimes the people greeted us with respect; sometimes they laughed at us. The news that a strange caravan was underway went before

St. Lucius (right) in Chur, Switzerland. The Redemptorists lived here in 1807.

us. When we arrived in a village, the people whispered to one another, "The Apostles are coming!" The children ran after us in droves as if we were interesting objects being offered for sale at the market. On our journeys we always followed the spiritual exercises prescribed by the Rule of our Order: meditation, rosary, breviary. In the afternoon we always kept strict silence for three hours. The most difficult part was the rising early for morning prayers. Even if we were very tired and had only slept a little, we were awakened at four A.M. Morning prayers always began on time."

After a dramatic crossing of the Grimsel pass in the middle of winter, the groups arrived in friendly Valais. The first group arrived in Visp on December 3. The international crew of twenty Redemptorists celebrated Christmas 1807 in their new Valais monastery.

Unfortunately, their peaceful stay in Visp would also not last very long. As early as November 1810, France annexed the Valais, and in 1812 Napoleon drove the Redemptorists out of the Valais. Some found sanctuary in Fribourg, and others continued to work scattered in parishes in the Upper Valais.[1]

Visp, Switzerland, at the beginning of the nineteenth century. The Redemptorists found accommodations here from 1807 to 1812.

Fatherly Concerns

Vicar General Hofbauer loved his colleagues. Their sufferings were his sufferings. The repeated expulsions of his brothers wore him down greatly. Although he was quite a sober man, he was not shy about expressing his own feelings to them. He wrote in a moving letter to his persecuted confreres in Switzerland: "I embrace all of you and hold all of you in my heart. Farewell, Brothers! You, my joy, my crown, my fame in Christ, the most beloved, farewell! May Jesus Christ fill you all with heavenly blessings. Redeem the world, dearest Brothers. The enemy cannot harm you, if Christ is with you. Pray for us as we pray for you and so that we may fulfill the most holy will of our Father."

This is language from a holy superior to whom spiritual leadership means more than just external organization! Clement is justifiably proud of his colleagues who have grown in Christ in the course of their way of the cross. Shortly after the expulsion of the Redemptorists from Chur, Hofbauer wrote to Superior General Blasucci: "With great joy, beloved father, you would recognize in them true sons of the Congregation who, having been tested in many trials, driven from country to country, have been found to be true and loyal martyrs of the Congregations."

Father Joseph Passerat (1772–1858), the superior with the knapsack (oil painting by Paul Deschwanden).

CHAPTER 22

Agenda for
a Death Sentence

I t did not take long before another crisis struck again. This
misfortune was even more difficult, more merciless, and more
destructive. An entire chain of events followed together to
cause the final demise of St. Benno. We can set forth in a kind of
agenda as to how Hofbauer's most difficult test came about—the
death sentence of St. Benno.

January 1808

The French Field Marshal Davoust, the new man in power in Warsaw, permitted the Bennonites to continue their work. Certainly,
everything did not run smoothly. Hofbauer writes: "The Jacobins
are spreading all kinds of terrible fairy tales about us....We have
been publicly threatened with the gallows." Despite these threats,
many things promised a hopeful future for the Bennonites. The ob-
servance of all sacraments increased daily in the church. Ten young
men were in the novitiate. Four more entered in a short time.

February 12

This fateful day bought a short report in the newspaper. Field
Marshal Davoust read it: it concerned a handful of monks who
are a danger to the community. These men have been expelled at

the request of the government of Bavaria—first from Babenhausen, then from Chur. The leader of this treasonous Order was an agitator in Warsaw. This newspaper article causes an avalanche of opposition. Davoust is taken aback. Monks—in Warsaw? So it's the Bennonites! Davoust seeks information from the Bavarian government.

March 13

Montgelas, the prime minister of Bavaria, and archenemy of the Redemptorists, replies. He repeats to his colleague Davoust the already well-known story: the Bennonites are Jesuits in disguise and close friends of the Bourbons, the dethroned French royal family. The subversively active monks turn the people into fanatics. They are a threat to the state. Their network of connections is very well-established and international.

The French secret police picks up the scent. The hunt begins. A search is made of the house at St. Benno. Harmless letters are discovered, and they are taken as "evidence of high treason."

April 12

Davoust informs Napoleon: "I am certain that these people are the enemies of every government, but especially of Your Majesty's. In their pamphlets they claim that Your Majesty wants to force the Pope to become Protestant....The Vicar General, Hofbauer, is an extremely dangerous man."

April 16

Today is the celebration of the Resurrection at the Easter Vigil. It is dark outside. French officers come to St. Benno. They behave improperly. The faithful defend themselves. There are wild scenes. The confrontations degenerate into violence. Both sides take this tumultuous riot as a provocation.

May 6

Davoust's report to Napoleon: "I would like to draw Your Majesty's attention to this association of extremely dangerous people. Majesty, these Redemptorists are your personal enemies." Around one hundred and fifty letters of the Bennonites are found and translated into French for Napoleon.

May 25

Napoleon writes: "Demand the expulsion of these monks from Warsaw. They are a rebirth of the Jesuits....Whatever one tells me of these priests—I believe they are capable of it. They harbor the greatest hatred for France." Thus the death sentence against St. Benno was pronounced. This directive was not changed by the final judgment of the specialist, who was supposed to investigate the one hundred and fifty letters for their treasonous content: "I have found no trace of politics....These 'Jesuits of Warsaw' are in no way mixed up in politics."

June 9

The decree of dissolution is ready to be signed: "The Bennonite monks must be removed from the borders of the Duchy of Warsaw immediately." At Napoleon's request, the man responsible, the King of Saxony, is forced to sign. It allegedly costs the King "tears to have to punish virtuous people with exile."

June 14

Field Marshal Davoust receives the decree of expulsion signed by the King. He writes to Napoleon: "The exile of this dangerous Congregation from the Duchy of Warsaw is a great relief because its members were the only men whom we really had to fear in our country."

The expulsion of the Bennonites from Warsaw. A malicious caricature drawn to inflame hatred against the Redemptorists in June 1808.

June 16

A strictly secret meeting of the ministry of police was held. A battle plan for the execution of the expulsion decree is drawn up: The time and manner of the operation are worked out to the last detail. Everything must remain secret.

The "strictly secret" plans are betrayed. A friendly police official comes in disguise to St. Benno. He warns Father Hofbauer: "The decree of expulsion has been signed. Careful, your house is already surrounded by secret police." And then the man disappears. Hofbauer and Jestershein gather the community in the dining room. The vicar general tells his brothers the terrible news. The news has the effect of a bomb. Helplessness, sobbing, crying.

But it is urgent. The attack could come at any moment. Measures are taken. The most valuable things are quickly hidden. Each man gathers a bundle of clothing and some travel money.

June 17

Things come to a head. Everything happens as it does in a raid. The streets are blockaded by the military. The commission charged with the suppression enters St. Benno. They herd the almost forty Bennonites together into one room. The church is closed and the house is locked. Then everything is expertly searched. Whatever appears suspicious is sealed by the police.

June 18–19

Endless interrogations, embarrassing searches are conducted. The officials attempt to alienate the younger Redemptorists from their Congregation through intimidation. Moral pressure is applied. They are supposed to sign a preprinted form. Only two declare their resignation from the Redemptorist community. All the others remain loyal. Persecution and exile are placed before disloyalty. There is even one unpleasant scene. A chamberlain wants to convince his own son to resign. All pleadings are in vain.

June 20

Monday at approximately four in the morning, wagons drive up. Soldiers guard the entire area. Thirty-seven Redemptorists wait in a small room—ready to travel. Now the commissioner calls each one by name. First six, then a further three are separated from the rest. The commissioner gives the remaining twenty-eight exact instructions. They will be divided into various coaches. Under the strictest military custody, one wagon after another drives away from St. Benno by different streets leading out of the city. An excited crowd of people awaits. Sobbing and lamentation can be heard everywhere. Moving scenes of departure take place. The Bennonites are brought to the fortress of Küstrin like hardened criminals.

St. Benno in War-
saw at the time of
St. Clement Maria
Hofbauer.

Then hatred celebrated its triumph. St. Benno, the bulwark against freethinkers in Warsaw, has fallen. The victors held a triumphal banquet on June 20 in the Masonic lodge. There were ecstatic raptures of hatred. As was odiously written later in a pamphlet: "Liguorians! No honest man speaks this word without a teeth-grinding curse; it should be sullied and branded for all time....The scattered members of the Liguorian society who had laid their cuckoo's egg in the nest of St. Benno are dispersed."

The people's anger did not cool for a long time. The military intervened against gatherings in the vicinity of St. Benno. Davoust had articles appear in the local press in order to justify the expulsion of the Bennonites. The Bennonites were accused of exerting their unholy influence on religion and morals; their supposed political actions and treasonous connections were pilloried. Statues and crucifixes at St. Benno were desecrated and even destroyed. None of this was likely to calm the angered population.

Even so, a song in praise of the expelled Bennonites was sung in the streets of Warsaw: a song which is still sung in Poland today.

CHAPTER 23

A Broken Heart

The wagons with the expelled Redemptorists arrived one after the other in Küstrin on the Oder. They were led to a barrackslike house. Each member of the group was given his own room. An altar was even set up in a large hall. The Bennonites were allowed to celebrate Mass daily. As had always been their custom, even the weekday Masses were celebrated with as much splendor as possible. There was also much singing. Mostly Protestants came in great numbers to listen to the singing and prayers of these strange monks.

Hofbauer had time to think in the fortress of Küstrin. What he had built over twenty years was now completely destroyed. With the loss of St. Benno came not only the loss of a house, a church, and a school—no, this meant the dissolution of his Congregation north of the Alps.

And yet Hofbauer remained quite calm. In his first letter from Küstrin he wrote: "We surrender ourselves to the fate that is given us by the will of God. It is sweet to suffer, because we have nothing for which we should reproach ourselves....God alone knows what fate awaits us....Through all this we recognize the will of God. May he be praised." The vicar general encouraged his colleagues "to keep up their spirits." They would later admit that Hofbauer's surrender to the will of God was contagious.

Hofbauer is said to have fallen ill during the flight from Küstrin to Vienna (July–September 1808). Countess Antonia Heyducki is supposed to have cared for him. As a sign of gratitude, Clement gave her this picture of the Madonna of Czestochowa. Today the picture hangs in the Redemptorist monastery of Leuk, Switzerland.

Into the Arms of the Police

Weeks passed. Then the hour of separation arrived. The imprisoned Bennonites were sent back to their homes in pairs. When

Hofbauer had to take leave of his beloved colleagues, he could no longer contain himself. He would often repeat later, "My heart was broken then." Did the saint imagine that he would never see most of them again in this life? His family was violently torn apart.

Hofbauer's chalice (Hofbauer Museum, Vienna).

His brothers were scattered to the four winds. All of them stood before an abyss and faced a completely unknown future. In his last letter from Küstrin, Clement wrote with great sadness: "A father is no longer allowed to remain among his sons; brothers are no longer permitted to live together."

Since Father Hofbauer was "the oldest of them all," he was accorded special treatment. The French authorities allowed him to take the young cleric Martin Stark as a traveling companion.[1] They received passports in which their exact prescribed travel route was listed.

An accident occurred on the journey. Martin lost the passports. When the refugees came across a military checkpoint, no one wanted to believe the story of the lost identity papers. The French commander believed them to be spies and wanted to have them executed. At the last minute, the commander decided to make inquiries at the fortress of Küstrin. In the meantime, he had the refugees held in captivity. After the information had arrived from Küstrin, they were given a sharp warning because they had strayed from the prescribed route. Then they were allowed to continue.

Near the end of 1808, the vicar general arrived in Vienna. Hofbauer, whom the Viennese would later name with pride the "Patron Saint of Vienna," was received accordingly. The official welcoming committee was there: the police. They welcomed the saint in their usual fashion: they arrested him, in fact as a suspected thief of church goods. When Clement Hofbauer was on his way to Vienna, the police discovered some church articles in his baggage that he had taken from St. Benno. This was reported to the police in Vienna. When the church property arrived in the city on the Danube, it was confiscated; and Hofbauer spent the first few days of his last stay in Vienna in a jail cell.

CHAPTER 24

Persecuted Prophets

A quiet sadness overcomes us when we take a bird's-eye view of this third stage in Hofbauer's life. The time frame from 1795 until 1808 was the time of Clement's great travels and his many attempts to establish a foundation of the Congregation. He went from country to country: from Poland to Switzerland, to Ermland (East Prussia), to Austria, Germany, France, and Italy. He wanted to travel even farther to Russia, to England, and to Canada. He almost always made these journeys on foot; usually they were very difficult and full of privations. In one place he became ill, in another he was thrown in jail. But everywhere some people admired and loved him. Others suspected, slandered, demonized, and persecuted him.

In many places, he tried to establish foundations of the Congregation. A few succeeded: in Mitau, Wollerau, Jestetten, Triberg, and Babenhausen. But these survived only a short time. Clement was fifty-seven when his greatest work—St. Benno—was destroyed and he himself was sent into exile. At this age successful men proudly point to all they have achieved and built. But Hofbauer's life's work lay completely in ruins when he landed in the arms of the Viennese police as a wanted refugee in September 1808. In truth, these were thirteen unsuccessful, wasted years. Everything had failed. And now he stood before the abyss. And we ask: why?

Zacharias Werner once dared to make the statement that there were three contemporary great men in Europe: Goethe, Napoleon, and Hofbauer. Goethe's world-view of "the purely human element" and Hofbauer's of the "purely Christian" were rather like antipoles. While Hofbauer had to go into exile because of his Christian convictions, Goethe celebrated great triumphs with his ideas. Napoleon and Hofbauer also "encountered" again and again without ever meeting each other personally. With a stroke of the pen the great Corsican and his minions destroyed Hofbauer's external work: in Babenhausen, Chur, Visp, and Warsaw. When Napoleon was dethroned and sent into exile in 1814, Hofbauer, whom he had banished into exile, was quietly pursuing his revival near St. Ursula's as the Apostle of Vienna. And we ask: wherein lay Hofbauer's greatness?

Clement Maria Hofbauer surely was tenacious and energetic, but he was neither a hero nor a genius nor a superman. He never surrendered to resignation in even the worst situations, but he broke down often. At these times, he lived only on the faith of a believer. In his life we discover a fundamental truth of the Bible: God wants to be strong and glorified in those who are weak.

"To preach the Gospel anew." Perhaps Clement preached the Gospel more through his life than his words. Or to say it another way: Saint Clement Maria Hofbauer had something of a prophet in him.

The Biblical Figure of the Prophet

The prophet is described in the Bible as a person of flesh and blood, but also as a man of God with a deep personal experience of God. He hears the call of God: "Go where I send you!" The prophet lets himself be taken by God and sent to his people. For him, meditating on the will of God and the salvation of the people are one and the same, because God defines himself as the Redeemer.

Thus prophets live the life of their people. They know and share the sufferings of their people. They stand up especially for the rights of the little people; and if their people are humiliated, they encourage and comfort them.

As a man of God and as a man of the people, the prophet is also forced to be man of his times, interpreting what are called the signs of the times in the light of God. If necessary, the prophet is the spokesperson of his people, and protests against everything in real life that does not conform to the spirit of God. Fearlessly, prophets become witnesses to God in a godless world. They censure the evils of the time in a prophetic tone and point to a future which belongs to God.

Precisely because they admonish people in God's name, prophets are persecuted, expelled, and killed by those who accuse them. The confessor, the witness to God, becomes a martyr.

This is how the Bible describes the shape and the life of a prophet.

Prophetic Traits in Hofbauer's Life: 1795–1808

Let us try to interpret Hofbauer's life in this sense and try to discover the "golden thread" that wove its way from his childhood and youth until this third stage in his life.

Man of God

Already as a hermit in Mühlfrauen and Tivoli, Hofbauer tried to become completely open to God, to experience him, and to discern his will. In the poverty of a hermitage, he learned to forsake the securities of this world and to entrust himself entirely to the care of the heavenly father. This "golden thread" weaves its way through Hofbauer's entire life.

During the years 1795–1808, Hofbauer stands out in so many ways. The constant separations correspond to a continual surrender of himself to God. He had barely established a house somewhere and made himself comfortable in this new spot when he had to fold his tent and move on into the unknown place without any security. Clement experienced this most bitterly when St. Benno was suppressed, and he was separated from his colleagues and sent into an uncertain exile.

He had had similar experiences earlier as a pilgrim. His many arduous journeys from 1795 until 1808 illustrate what the Church is: a wandering people who arduously follow the path of the pilgrim here on earth. "For here we have no lasting city, but we are looking for the city that is to come" (Hebrews 13:14).

Hofbauer let himself be seized, sent, and led by God. Even when Clement remained at a place for a short time, the faithful characterized him as a "man of God," as a man thoroughly dedicated to God. So it was in Jestetten and in Triberg and in Babenhausen. Everywhere he was called a saint.

Man of the People

The man of God showed himself to be a man of the people. The Redemptorist Hofbauer was close to the people his entire life. He especially loved children. He sought their salvation and achieved a measure of dignity and justice for them. The simple people, for their part, supported him everywhere; and sometimes they defended him angrily, even violently.

Man of His Time

Hofbauer was a man of his time. He did not flee from the Enlightenment, from the Illuminati (Rationalists), from freethinkers, from the French Revolution, from the away-from-Rome movement, from state-churchism, from political turmoils. Clement proved that one could experience God personally, even within a confused world. In his own fashion but always in the spirit of the Gospel, he tried to interpret the signs of the times.

He faced the concrete situation before him and saw in the events the will of God. In a dark hour when the last foundation in southern Germany was dissolved, he wrote: "Courage! God guides everything. In this hopeless situation I myself have surrendered myself to him entirely." In his darkest hour, when he was expelled from the Poland he loved so much, he found these words: "God no longer wants us here." Seeing the will of God in events means nothing more than saying "yes" to today because one believes that God is the ruler of history.

But Clement did not simply resign himself to events. Even a world which did not correspond to the Gospel was still for him "a sign of the times." God's principles are contrary to the principles of a godless world. Hofbauer exposed the evil of the times with prophetic courage; he dared to attempt to create a new future in the spirit of the Gospel.

Martyr

No wonder Hofbauer was hated and expelled time and again as "a very dangerous man" by those he attacked. Prophets are in fact persecuted. The abbot of Roggenburg hit the nail on the head when he wrote of Hofbauer and his colleagues: "They are working against the now prevailing spirit, the spirit of this world, so to speak. That is the entire crime for which they are being expelled." Prophets are persecuted and forced into martyrdom (Luke 13:34). "As they have persecuted me, so will they persecute you" (John 15:20). "Whoever wants to be my disciple, must pick up his cross and follow me" (Mark 8:34). Imitation of Christ, carrying the cross, persecution, martyrdom—these were Clement's guiding themes.

December 26 was Hofbauer's birthday and his baptismal day. On this day, Christendom celebrates the first martyr—the feast of Saint Stephen. Stephen is also the first patron of Vienna. Vienna and its Cathedral of St. Stephen play a large role in Hofbauer's life. One almost would like to think that God gave Clement his life's program with his birthday and baptismal day: to be a cross-bearer and a witness to Christ, that is, to be a martyr.

John was Clement's baptismal name. A deep friendship connected the evangelist and favorite apostle with the Savior. Christ was also a friend to John Hofbauer. Throughout his many sufferings, the Redemptorist Hofbauer bound himself to the person of the Savior. For his hermit name, the bishop gave him the name of a martyr, Clement of Ancyra.

How often the hermit Clement Hofbauer knelt before the statue of the Scourged Redeemer in Mühlfrauen. One could see that Hofbauer's life between the years 1795 and 1808 were a series of blows and scourges. During those years, Clement was severely scourged. The wound from one lashing had not even healed before the pain of the next lashing shuddered through him.

The Redemptorist Hofbauer saw the following of Christ as real missionary work for the Church. In a time of very severe distress, he wrote these strange words: "In persecution lies the divine majesty of his holy Church."

Part Four

Clement As the Apostle of Vienna 1808–1820

CHAPTER 25

Imperial City of Vienna

R ome, Warsaw, Vienna: three cities that are closely associated with the name of Clement Maria Hofbauer. Beautiful Vienna was and remains unique in the world. Both Johann Strausses celebrated the former residence of the Hapsburgs with justified pride: "There is only one Imperial City."

And there is only one Vienna in Hofbauer's life as well. This city on the blue Danube simply cannot be separated from the life of our saint. Clement was born barely sixty-two miles from Vienna; he was a baker's apprentice, a hermit, and a student in the vicinity. In the city, he worked as a baker, completed his studies, and formed the great friendships of his life with Hübl, Diessbach, Penkler, and others. From Rome and Warsaw, from Germany and Switzerland, he returned to Vienna time and again.

The Enlightenment

After being hunted for thirteen years, the saint, tired and harried, arrived in Vienna at the end of September 1808. He had planned to continue to another country after a brief stopover. But human beings propose and God disposes. During the last twelve years of his life, Hofbauer would not leave Vienna or its immediate surroundings. With his missionary sensibilities, he would discover the pastoral demands of a large city and develop a truly new type of pastoral work. It was in this way that he became the Apostle of Vienna.

We can only properly understand the many difficulties in his new apostolate and the greatness of his accomplishments against the historical background. At the beginning of the nineteenth century, Vienna had a population of about a quarter of a million people. According to baptismal records, approximately ninety-seven percent of Vienna's population were Catholic. But the state of religious life was not good. The anti-Church spirit of the Enlightenment and state churchism—the spirit of Josephinism—still reigned in Austria.

Clement Hofbauer lived in the century of the Enlightenment. It would be impossible to describe the essence of the Enlightenment in a few sentences without distorting it. This era released the almost unlimited forces of the human mind. Artists and scientists achieved great things. The great speed of progress in the natural sciences began the era of technology. This awakened an overly proud self-confidence in human beings who intoxicated themselves with their own abilities. Freedom and reason were writ inappropriately large and were often even revered. Humans proudly declared themselves the measure of all things.

This line of thinking was taken further with frightening logic by an extreme form of the Enlightenment. Soon it was said that every revealed faith—above all the Christian faith—was obsolete. Humanity had to be "enlightened." Whoever continued to believe was backward. Religious practices and piety were simply dismissed as fanaticism and zealotry. At the same time, the bitter struggle against the Christian world-view began, and the century of the Enlightenment ended in the blood-lust of the French Revolution.

Josephinism

The ideas of the Enlightenment also invaded state affairs. To be sure, the Church had overstepped its bounds in the past; it had often meddled in purely secular political affairs. There was a powerful reaction against this practice in many places during the eighteenth century. "Enlightened" sovereigns and magistrates attempted to free the state from all forms of tutelage to the Church. The state assumed the sovereignty of the Church. So-called state-churchism had as its goal the reduction of the rights of the Church or their complete suspension. The state was designated as the only source of law.

From 1765 to 1790, Catholic Austria was governed by Emperor Joseph II who, although a believer, was infected by the spirit of the Enlightenment. Especially after the death of his mother, the great Maria Theresa, the emperor consistently expanded the ideas of the Enlightenment and the sovereignty of the state into a system of state-churchism that was named "Josephinism" after him. He was surely not interested in destroying the Catholic Church, but was rather interested in church "reform" in the spirit of the Enlightenment. As a result, he achieved, in part, important and lasting improvements in the external organization of Church institutions. Unfortunately, Joseph II often let himself be influenced by anti-Church advisors. Imperial directives were aimed at reducing or entirely neutralizing the influence of the pope and the bishops. The priests were turned into civil servants.

The imperial directives also dared impertinent interferences in liturgical life. Everything was regulated—even the number of candles to be burned during Mass, and how often sermons could be given. In addition, innumerable declarations suppressed religious practices and popular piety. Processions and pilgrimages were forbidden, and popular devotions discouraged.

Such a policy toward the Church had to have devastating results. Along with the blurring of moral questions came a decline in morals. Soon no one felt comfortable in the monotony and coldness of such liturgical services. Thus the Catholic marrow was sucked from the bones of the faithful. Many felt alienated from the Church. The Church lost a large part of the intelligentsia. Even simple people could no longer find pleasure in their faith.

When Clement Hofbauer arrived in Vienna in 1808, the Catholic church in Austria was in a weakened state. The successors to Joseph II, Leopold II (1790–1792) and especially Emperor Franz I (1792–1835), tried to increase the influence of the Church through a series of directives and to repeal the worst Josephinist regulations. But these emperors were still surrounded by too many inveterate Josephinists: They barely succeeded with plans for a renewal. This contextual description is essential to understand Hofbauer's further activities in Vienna.

CHAPTER 26

The Tamed Saint

L et us return now to Clement Hofbauer. On his arrival in Vienna he was arrested as a suspected "church thief." Through the intervention of Bishop Hohenwart, he was released from jail after three days. But now that he had been caught in the wheels of the state police once, he was subsequently watched very closely.

First, Hofbauer had to find a lodging. His old friends and acquaintances did not abandon him. His former master-baker Weyrig provided him temporarily with a small apartment in the suburb of Alser. The "tamed" saint "who wanted to convert the entire world" now lived with his colleague Martin Stark in almost complete seclusion. The vicar general usually did his own cooking.

Hofbauer could not even think of any further travels because a bloody war raged again in the country. Napoleon laid siege to the city in May 1809. Two thousand eight hundred howitzers bombarded Vienna during the night of May 11. Clement experienced this night of horrors. Ferocious battles ensued. When the triumphant French emperor concluded a humiliating peace with the Austrians, there were tens of thousands of wounded in the military hospitals. Hofbauer helped out there, but otherwise he did not do much pastoral work.

Auxiliary Priest: 1809–1813

Baron Josef von Penkler was an influential personality in Austria at the time. The Castle of Mödling and the Fortress of Liechtenstein had belonged to him. Baron Penkler, Hofbauer's long-standing friend, was also the temporal administrator of the Minorite Church in Vienna. Penkler arranged a position as an auxiliary priest for his friend in this Italian national church. Hofbauer was given two rooms in the Foreigners' House: one for him and one for Martin Stark. He heard a rather large number of confessions, some in the Minorite Church, some in the former Capuchin monastery on the *Platzl* where Mechitarist monks (refugee Armenian monks) now lived. Otherwise he did not have much work. He was seldom allowed to preach.

Clement fulfilled these modest tasks as an auxiliary priest for about four years. This "creative pause" was a real gift for him. The former hermit was awakened in Hofbauer. Whenever he was not doing pastoral work, he prayed. He instinctively recognized in this contact with God that there was only one path for renewal in a Vienna contaminated by Josephinism: the path within, the path back to the middle and down into the deep.

At St. Ursula's (1813–1820)

Count Sigismund von Hohenwart, the Archbishop of Vienna, was very well disposed to our saint. The Ursulines had a large convent with a boarding school on Johannes Street. The emperor had called the sisters from Lüttich to Vienna in 1660. Soon the school was overcrowded. It had a good reputation, especially among the well-to-do and the aristocracy. When the spiritual director of the Ursulines died on April 3, 1813, the bishop named Clement Hofbauer confessor to the nuns and director of the church of St. Ursula. The duties of the new spiritual director consisted of hearing the sisters' confessions and seeing to the pastoral needs of the convent's church. He received a modest salary and free room and board as compensation.

The Ursulines owned a small, three-story apartment house in the *Seilerstätte* (the ropemakers' quarter) across from the convent. Hofbauer moved into his new apartment on July 18, 1813. He would live on the second floor of this apartment building for seven years, until his death. He had a room and a smaller anteroom. He reserved the third floor for one or more colleagues with whom he formed a community.

An appointment as confessor to the Ursulines, a new apartment: these were two events which certainly were not headline news in the Viennese press. But these two unlikely events mark a decisive turning point in Hofbauer's life and that of Austrian Catholicism. His room in the *Seilerstätte* would be many things in the future: a special kind of cloister, a private chapel, a meeting place for famous personalities, a confessional, an assembly room for panel discussions, a place from which missionary excellence would radiate, Hofbauer's study and the room where he would die—all in one! The saint now had his own house, his own pulpit, his church, and his confessional. This gave the brilliant pastor Hofbauer a chance to create an original kind of pastoral work masterfully adapted to the concrete situation he faced.

Hofbauer's bust in front of the Minorite Church in Vienna. Hofbauer worked as an auxiliary priest in this Italian national church from 1809 to 1813.

CHAPTER 27

Pastoral Work

B enevolence and sympathy are the ground rules for every kind of pastoral work. Sympathy means "human beings feeling for one another," being benevolently interested in the concrete person, loving the individual the way he or she is— along with each person's worries and hopes. Hofbauer's pastoral work in Vienna was exactly that: a truly "human" one because as a priest he was a brother to innumerable people.

Spiritual Guide and Secular Advisor

Hofbauer began the reform of the Church from within with surprisingly multifaceted, small projects. He achieved most conversions as a confessor. Clement possessed a special charisma for this form of individual pastoral work. He often sat for hours on end in the confessional, to the point of exhaustion, until he collapsed into unconsciousness. Even in the middle of winter, he had the night watchman wake him as early as three or four in the morning. He then went out in prayer and contemplation to the Capuchin church on the *Platzl*. Usually there were already penitents waiting for him. From there he returned to the church of the Ursulines where his confessional was surrounded daily. Many even made their confessions in his apartment.

Hofbauer became the spiritual guide and secular advisor to people from all of the professional and social classes. His penitents included aristocrats, civil servants, intellectuals and artists,

bishops and university professors, rich and poor. The list of famous names is long: Friedrich and Dorothea Schlegel, Adam
Müller, Friedrich Klinkowström, Friedrich and Sophie Schlosser,
and so on. The crown prince and later king, Ludwig of Bavaria,
chose Father Hofbauer as his Father confessor during his stay in
Vienna. A persistent grapevine sprang up in Vienna. One penitent called on another. Through students he converted still more
students, through craftsmen he brought other craftsmen to his
side, through civil servants other civil servants, through children
the parents, through wives husbands and thus he converted entire families, always moving slowly and quietly. In ever-widening
circles, Clement's influence spread imperceptibly, like a soft breeze.

Hofbauer's pastoral work in the confessional and in his one-
on-one conversations had a broad and deep effect. The famous
dramatist and convert Zacharias Werner admitted, for example:
"I only became truly Catholic through Hofbauer." Hofbauer's
success lay in his spiritual guidance. He instructed a respectable
number of enthusiastic Christians who would in turn become the
forerunners of Church reform and the popular Christian movement in Austria. The enemies of the Church realized full well the
dangers of this apostolate. We read in a police report that zealous
piety was in fashion once again and on the daily agenda: "The
confessional is the most powerful means for maintaining this newest fashion." What then was the secret of this confessor?

Ways of the Heart

Hofbauer's knowledge of people and the instinctive perception
with which he saw into the most secret corners of the heart amazed
everyone. "He could read the hearts of people; the secrets of the
heart were open to him." Zacharias Werner expressed it meta-
phorically: "Hofbauer sees through planks."

The secret of his successes surely lies still deeper. Father
Madlener, a penitent and friend of the saint, was doubtless correct when he said: "His knowledge of human nature in the confessional was wonderful; it was not a result of art but rather a gift
from above." During confession or in a pastoral dialogue, he
seemed to be completely absorbed in God. Thus his advice came

from deep within. "He listened for a while with closed eyes, then he opened his eyes for a moment and very calmly spoke ten to twelve words which contained everything that the questioner needed to know." He did not need hours of useless talk in order to help an individual. Each of his words appeared to find its way deep into the soul and left behind a powerful impression.

Everyone felt that Hofbauer did not want to bind people to him but rather to bring them into contact with God. Maria Rizy, a niece of the well-known dramatist Franz Grillparzer, reported that whenever Hofbauer was pressed for time, he very calmly ended the confession with the saying: "What I cannot tell you, the Holy Spirit will provide." Certainly he himself tested what he repeatedly advised others: "It is better to speak to God about the sinner than with a sinner about God."

Taking Each Individual Seriously

Hofbauer encountered each individual with benevolence, felt his way into each one's world of thought, and treated each person as an individual. This approach may have been the third secret of this very successful confessor. Today we would call Hofbauer a talented psychotherapist.

He believed in the good in people and strove to awaken the noble within them: "Our mistakes should humble us but not make us despondent." He tirelessly invited his penitents to trust him and to be joyful. One of his favorite sayings in the confessional was: "Diligently remember the word of the Lord: There will be more joy in heaven over one sinner who has repented than over ninety-nine righteous people who do not need to repent." Then again he said: "Let yourselves fall into the mercy and the will of God as a stone lets itself fall into water. We want to behave with God as a child with its mother."

He was especially kind to those who failed. "He hated the Jansenist discipline." He made confession easy for those who were lost. A very beautiful text describes his method: "He was a born confessor for lost sons and daughters whose shame stopped the words on the tip of their tongues. In such cases, he only said these words: 'Continue; I already know what you want to say.'"

He had a special knack for handling overly scrupulous people. His methods were occasionally quite strange. A timid priest was taking a long time to clean the chalice and paten. Hofbauer went up to him, blew on the paten and said: "Leave something for the angels to do." As the spiritual advisor to certain overly scrupulous people, Clement needed much patience and strong nerves. A Viennese man by the name of Kraus made many demands on Clement. Hofbauer commented moodily: "One Kraus I can handle, but two of them would kill me."

One of the Poor

Clement Hofbauer is considered quite rightly to be a man of the people. Wherever he could, he stood on the side of the little person. This stance is another golden thread that is woven through his entire life. His love for the unfortunate in Vienna became proverbial.

The poor districts of Vienna were found mainly in the suburbs. Hofbauer went almost daily on foot to these slums. He carried food and clothing under his broad coat for his regulars. Gradually this priest with the bulging cloak simply became part of the cityscape. Among the circle of his penitents and friends, he organized a quiet resistance against poverty and suffering. He himself was only one among many other helpers.

But charity is an art. There are benefactors who understand perfectly how to shame, to wound, or to make the needy dependent upon them with their small gifts. Clement Maria Hofbauer was not one of these people. For example, Hofbauer did not simply give alms to the painter Natter, who found himself in great need; instead he commissioned paintings so that the artist could earn a living by his own efforts. One of these paintings is still to be found today in the Redemptorist monastery of Maria-am-Gestade in Vienna. He even made attempts to change unjust social structures.[1]

A Refuge for Beggars

And then the saint had another idea. Typical Hofbauer! In many reports from the time we read the following: "He regularly had penniless and poor guests at his home for dinner." Clement was still vicar general of the Redemptorists. His monastery on the *Seilerstätte* was not large. Usually only two or three colleagues lived there with him. Then Hofbauer, the superior of the Congregation, dared something outrageously bold: the poor were allowed to be guests in this house. The dinner table of his small community became a meeting place for the poor. At lunchtime, the room was sometimes full of poor soldiers, poor students, and beggars. He served them himself. He ate a little something while he worked. Clement Maria Hofbauer, the "saint without a miracle," as he has been called, appears to have worked miracles after all. Many reliable witnesses have reported that Hofbauer often multiplied bread and other kinds of foods.

Like One of Them

What this brotherly saint did for the poor is not what is most surprising, but rather what he was among them. His solidarity with the needy connected him to the fate of the poor. His apartment and food were extremely modest. His clothes were clean but worn, and he usually mended them himself. Hofbauer's willingness to accept uncertainty and his evangelical patience became a sign of hope for many. "He relied entirely on providence." He lived as a poor man among the poor, and he shared with them whatever he had. As humorous as he was, he could joke: "I have already become very poor but not so poor that I could not give something."

Clement was closely connected to those people who lived unnoticed on the edges of society. Thus it is no wonder that he did not strive for earthly honors, but rather loathed the glitter and lofty character of the world. Those missionaries are believable who emphasize being among the people as much as the effect they may have upon them!

Among the Dying and Disheartened

The poor have many faces, and suffering has many names. Some of them are sickness, death, and despair.

Clement Hofbauer was often called to the sick and the dying in Vienna no matter what the weather. He is supposed to have ministered to over two thousand dying people in those twelve years. Whenever it involved so-called difficult cases, he preferred to go on foot. He prayed the rosary on the way. He said he didn't know of a single sinner who had not repented if he had had enough time to pray the rosary on the way.

Hofbauer was very good to the sick. He liked to bring flowers or some other small gift to cheer them up. Whenever things got serious, he would use his own methods. One day he was summoned by a nobleman who had not confessed in a long time. When the deathly ill man saw the priest, he became raving mad. The anger awoke new strength in him. Cursing and swearing he showed Hofbauer the door. Hofbauer asked him calmly whether he had already made the necessary arrangements for the great journey into eternity. The man continued to swear: "Get out! Go! Leave me alone!" Hofbauer moved away. At the door he stopped and looked at the man in the bed for a while without speaking. The man shouted: "What do you want now? Go away!" And the saint answered calmly: "No, I will go no further. It is almost over with you. And just once I would like to see a damned man die." That worked. The dying man asked: "Father, can you forgive me?" Crying with remorse, the man confessed. In gratitude, he pressed a crucifix and the hand of the saint to his chest. And he died.

Angel of Comfort

Hofbauer always had the right words of comfort for the mourners where death took its toll. We find one example among many in a letter from Josef Pilat: "My Franz died today between one and two A.M....My wife is suffering greatly....Father Hofbauer has appeared to us like an angel of comfort." How human pastoral work can be!

When Life Breaks People

Many people are hit hard by life. That fact is certain. And not all of them are strong enough for the burdens of life. That is also certain. Many are saved if they meet the right advisor. Clement Hofbauer apparently had the talent with just one gesture to give back the courage to live to certain suicidal people.

There was a rich noble lady. Through inflation she lost her wealth. She fell into despair and wanted to jump into the river. Clement hurried to her. After a short conversation, he bent down, picked up a handful of earth: "What is money? A handful of dust." She became his penitent, and a new joy in life awoke within her.

One evening, Clement was walking along the Danube with some friends. A man walked past. Hofbauer instinctively followed the despondent man, greeted him in a friendly manner, and offered him his tin of tobacco: "May I offer you some snuff?" After a longer discussion he invited the man home with him, and this man began a new life. These are only some of many other similar examples.

CHAPTER 28

Preaching the Gospel Anew

In addition to his one-on-one pastoral work and his work in the confessional, Clement Hofbauer found the Mass and preaching to be the most effective means for renewing people's faith and achieving Church reform.

The church of the Ursulines in Vienna was not well known and not well attended until 1813. Sermons were held at the most at Christmas, Easter, and Pentecost. Almost no one came to the Sunday Masses. Then Father Hofbauer was named director of the Church of St. Ursula. He created a small sensation on the first Sunday. Clement asked when the sermon would be. The nuns were at a loss: "What? A sermon? But how? They are forbidden. And there are no listeners." To the astonishment of the sisters, Father Hofbauer put himself above the Josephinistic rules for the Mass and climbed up into the pulpit. Soon the church was jammed full every Sunday with people of different classes and professions. A report by the indignant police speaks of "quite a dreadful crowd."

Most Splendid Mass in All Vienna

The cold, emotionless Mass of the Josephinistic era had starved the religious life of the faithful. Hofbauer ignored the state's prescriptions. He brought flowers and candles into the church, arranged for beautiful music and singing, held devotions and processions, introduced the Forty Hours Devotion and visits to the Blessed Sacrament. A respectable number of altar boys gathered around the altar. His Mass servers were not just boys but also students and men of all classes. The faithful people were happy that they were allowed to celebrate their faith again. And many came to St. Ursula's because "the most splendid Mass in all of Vienna" was celebrated there.

Reformer of the Sermon

Saint Clement Hofbauer, the missionary, set great store by the sermon. The famous student of Hofbauer and preacher at the cathedral, Dr. Emanuel Veith, reports: "I heard him say these splendid and emphatic words very often, yes, almost daily: 'The Gospel must be preached anew!' A large commentary could be written about that one phrase." And, in fact, people have wondered a great deal about this word *anew*. Does it mean again, or in a new way? What's the difference? Both are included in it. A very important document by Vicar General Hofbauer reads: "As regards the sermon, one must pay particular attention to appeal to the people and to make a true proclamation of the Gospel."[1] These are the two keys to understanding Hofbauer's reform of the sermon and to its success—the true Gospel and popular appeal.

The True Gospel

In contrast to so many fashionable preachers of the time, the saint went back to "the true Gospel." We possess neither a sermon nor an outline of a sermon by him. We do know, however, the main themes of his preaching: the love and mercy of God, Jesus Christ the Savior, the Catholic Church, repentance and faith. Thus he preached the great truths of the faith, but he also scourged the "evil customs, the mistakes and vices of the world." Police informants who had to monitor Hofbauer's sermons at St. Ursula's reported: "He is a zealous conveyor of the living faith, not a preacher of morals but rather of dogma; he attempts to work through emotions rather than through the mind; his proofs are not based on reason, but rather on the texts of the Bible and their exegesis and application....His sermons are pure exegesis of the Gospel or extemporaneous homilies." Hofbauer's manner of preaching can hardly be described more precisely than in these words.

Popular Appeal

Hofbauer himself formulated just what he meant by popular appeal: "The word of God must be preached so that everyone understands it, little people and important people, the learned and the ignorant. And this is also our founder's instruction." The saint endeavored diligently to achieve this closeness to the people. He often began his sermons with these words: "Today I want to speak so simply and clearly that each elderly mother and also the children will understand me." And, in fact, he did preach in an extremely plain and simple manner. He loathed high and mighty speeches without any scriptural references, as well as everything artificial, affected, and farfetched. Hofbauer was not a blusterer in the pulpit. Instead, his sermons took the form of a heartfelt dialogue. In the middle of the lecture, he could turn directly to the listeners with a question, an aside, a prayer, or a joke. He was not a humorless preacher of morals and repentance. No, Clement was praised for his "geniality, cheerfulness and joviality."

He was not a born public speaker, and his German was far from perfect. His preaching technique betrayed many flaws, so that his friends often asked him to exercise a little more care in the form of his sermons.

Effect of Hofbauer's Sermons

The effect and success of Clement's sermons stood in no relation to the rhetorical means at his disposal. He exuded a real magical power. His listeners very often broke into loud weeping from the strong emotion he aroused. The people said to one another: "We have never heard such a preacher" or "One word from his lips lasts me an entire week."

A force emanated from him that the greatest sinners could not withstand. Johann Petrak, who later became a Redemptorist himself, tells of his experience of Hofbauer's preaching and his conversion: "At the time I was studying philosophy at the university of Vienna. According to my beliefs, I was a freethinker. One day, an acquaintance invited me to a sermon by Father Hofbauer who counted very many university students among his listeners. I did not want to go at any price. I had not seen the inside of a church in a very long time. But since the pressure became annoying, I gave in and went along. When we arrived, the church was already packed. I was glad to have to remain at the back because that way I had the best opportunity for quickly leaving without being seen. But soon I was completely caught up in the power of the preacher's words. I just stood there and listened. Suddenly I felt a pain in my neck. I wanted to rub it but could not. Strange! I was so carried away by his words that I had involuntarily pushed my way through the crowd so that I stood directly in front of the pulpit, my head held high so that I could see the speaker."

After the sermon, the people who wanted to go to confession usually came into the sacristy. He always accepted them lovingly. Clement used to say: "One must forge the iron while it is hot and pliable. At the pulpit, one must shake loose the nuts from the tree forcefully and in the confessional one must collect them gently."

Naturally, this phenomenon cannot be explained. Generally, some people were convinced at the time that hearers were swept away by Hofbauer's sermons because of the unwavering power of his faith and also because of the special spiritual talent of this man of God.

A friend of Hofbauer's provides us with some explanation for the secret of such successful sermons: Clement could have said as the Apostle John did: "I proclaim what I have heard, what I have seen and witnessed with my eyes, what I have touched with my hands." Clement's preparations for the sermons was the following. He entered the person of the Savior and his Gospel through love. "His preparation was simple, the book that he studied with extraordinary diligence was his crucified Savior and Lord." At the beginning of the week, he had a passage read from Sunday's Gospel reading. After a few words he said: "*Sufficit*. That's enough." During the week he immersed himself in this Bible passage through prayer.

Clement once asked one of his pupils what the best preparation for a sermon was. Without waiting for the answer he slapped

his knee, as if to say that one must prepare a sermon on one's
knees.

"The Word of God Is Not in Chains"

In conclusion, we can hear as representative of so many witnesses the judgment of two perceptive and highly regarded spir-
ited people:

> *Sophie Schlosser:* Early today I heard Father Hofbauer
> preach in the church of the Ursulines. His speech moved
> me and pleased me greatly....Such sermons cannot but
> have a great impact on the hearts of the listeners....The
> speeches of this man are so completely different from all
> the others that one hears....I have never seen a man who
> knew how to make one love Christianity as he does. Dur-
> ing his sermons I often think that the Apostles must have
> spoken this way.

> *Johannes Pilat:* I myself have heard learned and educated
> men say: If you want to hear a good speaker go to this or
> that church. But if you want to hear an apostle then go to
> the Ursuline church to hear Father Hofbauer.

He preaches as one who has power. The power of his sermons
came from the force of his faith, which was ingrained in him and
expressed itself in every characteristic of his face, in all his gestures. E.g., he spoke of Christ becoming a man: "He became flesh,"
and he clapped his hands together. These simple words, spoken
with such apostolic conviction and powerful action made a powerful impression on all his listeners and especially on me, and destroyed all doubt."

Hofbauer hit the state-churchism of Josephinism right in the
heart with such pastoral work. The secret agents spied on him,
but the police had great patience. At a certain point, however,
these "too strongly missionary sermons" could no longer be accepted or tolerated. The state police succeeded in getting an in-
junction against Father Hofbauer's preaching. The saint was sen-

tenced to silence from September 24, 1815, until October 1816. The friends of the saint were very sad and bitter at this.

The pulpit at St. Ursula's in Vienna.

CHAPTER 29

Hofbauer and Youth— Charisma of Humanity

I f the education of faithful layperson was a constant in Hofbauer's pastoral work, he always remained extraordinarily adaptable in his methods. He did not simply copy in Vienna what he had done very successfully in Warsaw. When he went into exile to Austria in 1808, he found there a completely new situation. Almost completely separated from the community of his Order, he could hardly count on the help of his brothers. He counted on the laity for his reform work. In addition, he was followed and spied upon at every turn by the Austrian secret police in the city on the Danube. An organized lay apostolate was unthinkable under these circumstances. Thus Hofbauer dared to undertake new initiatives in his pastoral work. We may call his intuition and his courage astounding. In small cells with informal groups, he began work that constantly grew.

Each Day—An Open House

Clement had always been a man born to friendship. His small monastery in Vienna now became an open house always and to everyone. Even when he himself was not at home, anyone could enter this small monastery, which was without locks or supervision. In Vienna, the saint built his pastoral work on friendship and hospitality. Thus he often invited people home with him: "Why don't you come to lunch today?" And he was genuinely happy when someone visited him. This way Hofbauer's little house gradually became a religious center of Vienna, radiating a missionary energy without equal. Prelates and artists, poor people and aristocrats, soldiers and professors, visited the simple Redemptorist there. Above all, his apartment became a meeting place for youth, especially university students.

Hospitality—A Gesture of Humanity

The hospitality that we are talking about here naturally did not consist of organizing the most expensive banquets possible. There were no exquisite foods and expensive wines, no splendid salons with soft upholstered furniture at Hofbauer's apartment. He doubtless offered his young guests some small refreshment. He always had some fruit, baked goods, or cold dishes in his large cupboard. Hospitality also needs visible signs and expressions of affection. The most important thing, however, was that youth could experience a lot of true humanity in Hofbauer's house. Their own admissions are numerous: "They were allowed to visit him in his room as often as they wished. They were never unwelcome; he always had time to receive them no matter how busy or ill he was." He always created the impression "that he had expected them....He always received them with the same tenderness, never showed in the least that they were an annoyance at the time."

Hofbauer discovered the way to youth remarkably quickly. He did not need any pastoral tricks. He was simply their priestly friend. And they could not resist his attractive power. They felt that here was a priest who understood us, who took each person seriously, "as if he were the only one." Three snapshots of Hofbauer's time in Vienna serve to illustrate his method.

One evening, Clement was not yet in his room. The students present got into an argument. Some of them came down hard on the eighteen-year-old Kosmaček and called him a heretic because he defended his own particular ideas. Hofbauer appeared in the middle of this scene. When he learned what was going on, he said: "Leave him in peace." Then he hugged the vexed young man and patted him in a friendly way.

The famous writer Zacharias Werner visited our saint often. Whenever he found the house bursting with young people, annoyed, he could scold angrily: "These young bucks are always here." Then Clement answered roguishly: "I prefer these young bucks to you."

Clement could sympathize delicately with the personalities of young men. He allowed everyone to be himself and did not treat them all the same way. There is the story of Franz Hätscher, who later became a priest and a Redemptorist. He had caused his mother a great deal of anguish. One day the scoundrel arrived in church by chance. Hofbauer's sermon shook him so severely that he wanted to confess immediately after the Mass. The saint took him by the hand and said to him: "You want to confess already? No, come with me." The young penitent stayed in Hofbauer's apartment for several days. Each day the saint showed him a picture of Jesus at the whipping post. "Franz," he said to him, "learn your lesson there." Then he left the penitent alone with the Man of Sorrows. After Franz had made his confession, the saint invited Franz's mother to breakfast, and there was a great reconciliation between mother and son.

Hospitality Is Pastoral Care

Youth felt themselves drawn to the apartment house in the *Seilerstätte* as if pulled by a magnet. Why? We are faced with a puzzle. It is certain that the *presence of the saint* attracted them. The decisive element was not what Hofbauer said to them but rather what he was for them.

How strange! The encounter with the saint became a happy experience of faith for young people. Their reports leave no doubt about that: "These visits seemed to me like my own Sunday at home." "Everyone felt happy in his presence, happy to be able to speak to him." These meetings possessed something of the atmosphere of the original Church, which also met in "house churches." These meetings are referred to as *familia sacra*, as a holy union. No less a person than the well-educated Sophie Schlosser dared to admit the following: "I have never spent happier hours than when we had breakfast with him as we often did after Mass where we had taken Communion. Here, surrounded by his pupils who served us, he was the merriest, really most child-like, happiest father of the house."

A despicable police report suspected scandals because women were seen going in and out of Hofbauer's house. This report culminated in the amazing claim that the success of these meetings "expresses itself in such a conspicuous manner that those who take part in them appear completely transformed."

These transformed people were infected with Hofbauer's missionary spirit and in turn became apostles. A university student who was there formulated it as follows: Hofbauer's disciples did what the disciples of Jesus did: one called the other. "If one had come to know Father Hofbauer, he had no peace until he had brought some of his fellow pupils to him....We felt an uncommonly great joy whenever we learned that this person or that person had been to see Father Hofbauer, because we took that person for converted. We had such a high opinion of Father Hofbauer."

Discussion Groups

Hofbauer's house, thus, gradually became a meeting place for young people. Many of them had chosen Father Hofbauer as a confessor and advisor. They came to his apartment to confess or simply to get advice. Some came occasionally, others almost every day.

This is how the well-known evening gatherings came about. During the last years of his life, this circle of faith became a regular part of the saint's pastoral program. Whenever he returned home late from visiting the sick, the room was usually full of young people. Then Hofbauer would mumble to himself: "Beautiful little people! Beautiful little people!"

These evenings were quite spontaneous. There was no planning, no agenda. Everything happened in a relaxed manner. Each meeting developed differently. Sometimes it was a kind of forum for a discussion of religious topics or questions about the Church. Others were similar to today's Bible classes or prayer meetings. One evening there was an exchange of faith experiences; on another, someone read aloud from a book. Hofbauer brought up his own concerns just like the others.

Sometimes he left the young people alone while he heard confessions in the next room or prepared his next sermon. If the noise was too great, Hofbauer fought it in his own fashion. In order to muffle the sound, the saint put a black cloth over his head.

Sometimes Hofbauer took an evening stroll through the city with his restless horde. At other times, he organized something like a pilgrimage for the young people.

Many of these young scholars went to Mass every day. All this created quite a stir. This rapid change in the attitudes of the students was "a miracle of grace."

Gradually, a smaller group developed within this larger circle around Hofbauer. Those students most willing to learn let themselves be educated and molded by Hofbauer, and they were always men of stature who would later play an important role in the Church and society.[1] "They looked upon him as a father." Examples of such a following are rare indeed.

CHAPTER 30

The Hofbauer Circle

In Vienna, as in other cities at the time, intellectual life was mainly fostered in groups of people who held membership in the same social class, or through circles of friends. Clement Hofbauer especially exploited circles of friends for his apostolate. It was in and through such circles that he attempted to function as a missionary. Men and women, young people and the elderly, nobility and bourgeoisie, academics and artists, civil servants and prelates, students and professors, belonged to Hofbauer's circle. Therein lies the amazing thing, that so many people from all social classes, but especially leading personalities, gathered around this simple priest. They entrusted themselves to his leadership, accepted his spirit, and carried it further.

Many of Hofbauer's penitents and friends knew one another. They formed different groups of friends among themselves. Gradually the saint became the actual focal point of these informal groups. His influence succeeded in making them into the starting points of a new spiritual attitude. This strange network of connections surrounding the Apostle of Vienna is usually called the "Hofbauer Circle." Sometimes, the term "Romantic Circle" is used because Hofbauer met more or less regularly with famous Romantics (Zacharias Werner, Clemens Brentano, Josef Eichendorff, and so on) in the houses of Friedrich Schlegel or Adam Müller and in the salon of the so-called "*Stroblkopf* Society."[1] If one asks, however, why these scholars, poets, artists, and diplomats felt drawn to Clement, one is faced with another puzzle as to why Hofbauer was accepted as the advisor, the confessor, and friend of leading Romantics and politicians! It would be worthwhile discussing the relationships of the saint to some of the more or less well-known people of his circle in detail. But that would go beyond the limits of this book. We will confine ourselves to a brief description of some of the families from Hofbauer's circle.

Portraits of Families From the Hofbauer Circle: Friedrich Schlegel's Family

Friedrich Schlegel (1772–1829): Son of a Protestant minister, Friedrich Schlegel studied law and then literature. A language scholar, German poet and academic, he was the founder and theoretician of the Romantic School. He was also known as the "Prince of the Romantics." In 1808, he and his companion Dorothea Mendelssohn converted to Catholicism. They were married in the Church and took up residence in Vienna. Baron Penkler introduced the Schlegel family to Father Hofbauer. The saint became their confessor and fatherly friend. "As an almost daily visitor to the house," Hofbauer exerted the greatest influence upon Friedrich and Dorothea. "Both were attached to him with an unlimited love and respect," Dorothea's son, Philipp, admitted. Friedrich permitted himself to call the saint "old man Hofbauer." For his part, Clement could embrace his friend after a disagreement and say to him: "You are really my Friedrich."

The Schlegel house became the headquarters of the Catholic Romantic Movement. Hofbauer met many poets and writers there and exerted a great deal of influence over them.

Friedrich Schlegel (1772–1829). The German poet and academic was a very close friend of Father Hofbauer.

Dorothea Schlegel (1763–1839): Friedrich's wife was the daughter of the Jewish philosopher Moses Mendelssohn. She was one of the great women of the Romantic Movement in Vienna. She also chose Hofbauer to be her confessor and spiritual guide.

Philipp Veit (1793–1877) and Johannes Veit (1790–1854): They were Dorothea's sons from her first marriage. Both became painters. In 1810, Hofbauer prepared them for conversion. Baron Penkler was their godfather. They later went to Rome, where they joined the Luikas Society and the so-called "Nazarene" school of art. Hofbauer's spirit continued to influence them. He also dared to evaluate their works critically: "The mother of Jesus appears to be too much like a nun." The Veit brothers maintained a warm friendship with Father Hofbauer for his entire life.

Adam Müller's Family

Adam Müller (1799–1829): He was surely the most well-rounded individual of the Catholic Romantic Movement and the Hofbauer Circle: a natural scientist, philosopher, political economist, historian, and man of letters. This Protestant academic became a Catholic in 1805–1806 and an active lay apostle. In 1811, he came to Vienna and met Hofbauer. Clement became his confessor, advisor, and friend. Through his speeches and his literary works, Müller achieved a great many things for the reform movement in Vienna. He died in 1829 in the arms of his friend Friedrich Klinkowström. Müller's assessment of Hofbauer is significant: "Strange, that despite the homeliness of this man, he exudes so much authority."

Adam Heinrich Müller (1779–1829) was the most important social scientist of the Romantic Period and a close collaborator of Hofbauer.

Sophie Müller (1775–1849): She was Adam's wife and was accepted into the Catholic Church by Hofbauer.

Friedrich von Klinkowström's Family

Friedrich Klinkowström (1787–1835): He studied art, became a painter, and was also numbered among the Romantics. One event seems to have had a deep effect upon him. As a youth, he and a few friends went to a shady tavern. The atmosphere was wanton. Then a prostitute began dancing. Friedrich was suddenly shocked. Close to the seductive girl, he had a vision of a priest who was looking at Friedrich as if to warn him. The boy shuddered to his very marrow. He left the tavern as fast as possible. At home he took a piece of paper and painted the apparition. Years passed. In 1812, Klinkowström went to the Minorite Church with his friend Friedrich Schlegel. He flushed. At the altar, he saw the priest who had warned him with a glance in that tavern near Hamburg.

Another encounter with Hofbauer made an impression on him. Friedrich Klinkowström told a silly joke about religion and salvation at a pleasant gathering in the presence of Hofbauer. The saint reprimanded him harshly: "Sir, what you are laughing at cost a lot of blood of the most precious kind."

In 1814, Hofbauer would welcome him into the Catholic Church and become his confessor and advisor. For his part, Klinkowström became Hofbauer's pupil and closest colleague. The saint often visited him in his home.

Louise Klinkowström-Mengershausen († 1821): Friedrich's wife Louise was the sister of Elise, the wife of Josef von Pilat. In 1814, the three Mengershausen sisters converted to Catholicism. Hofbauer became their father confessor.

Josef von Pilat's Family

Josef von Pilat (1782–1865): Josef von Pilat was a writer and a civil servant who also served as private secretary to Prince Metternich from 1801. Later he became Court secretary and government advisor in the chancellery. A Freemason and a favorite of both

Metternich and the emperor, von Pilat held an influential position. Through his wife, he met Father Hofbauer in 1814. Then he left the Freemasons, converted, and became a zealous Catholic and a thoroughly active lay apostle. Josef confessed: "I owe my conversion to the Catholic faith and life to Hofbauer's efforts. He became my confessor. Outside the confessional I spoke to him at least twice weekly." As editor of the *Österreichischer Beobachter*, Josef von Pilat edited this official paper according to Hofbauer's principles.

Elise von Pilat-Mengershausen (1786–1829): Converted through Hofbauer's influence, she also became his penitent. Her house was a gathering place of leading Catholic politicians and civil servants around Hofbauer. Clement also instructed Josef and Elise's children in religion. Aloysia became a nun and Johannes a Redemptorist.

The Friedrich Schlosser Family

Friedrich Schlosser (1776–1861): From a famous patrician family in Frankfurt, Friedrich Schlosser was related to Goethe. A German historian, he was also a philologist, writer, and translator.

He arrived in Vienna in late autumn 1814 as Frankfurt's representative to the Congress of Vienna. He met Hofbauer in Pilat's house. He and his wife asked to be accepted into the Catholic Church. Under Hofbauer's influence, Friedrich Schlosser opposed Wessenberg's plan at the Congress of Vienna for a German National Church. His house became a focal point of the Catholic Restoration.

Sophie Schlosser (1786–1865): Friedrich's refined and highly educated wife had a great influence in society. After her conversion, Hofbauer became her confessor. She would later write the pope about all she owed to Father Hofbauer.

The Franz von Széchényi Family

Franz von Széchényi (1754–1820): A Hungarian politician, he was a Privy Councilor, and a Knight of the Golden Fleece. He was one of the most respected men of his country. He was also an art collector and founder of the Hungarian National Museum. He resigned from all of his positions due to health reasons and came to Vienna in 1811. In 1814, he purchased a palace which soon became the main meeting place of the Hofbauer circle. Father Hofbauer and other guests were invited to lunch Wednesdays and Fridays. They especially discussed issues of church politics there. This Széchényi Club was an annoyance to the police. For that reason it was carefully watched. Hofbauer was recognized as the driving force of this circle: "No one can understand how this dangerous man can be tolerated here any longer: he is a passionate supporter of the Roman *curia*."

Juliana Széchényi: Together with her husband, Franz, she generously supported the poor sponsored by her confessor Clement. Hofbauer instructed her children in religion, Franziska, Sophie, and Stephan. Stephan Széchényi (1792–1860) became one of the most powerful men of his country; he was called simply the "Great Hungarian."

Julie Zichy (1790–1816): The niece of Count Franz Széchényi was one of the most distinguished women of the aristocracy at the time. She was, as it were, the star of the Congress of Vienna; emperors and kings worshipped and adored her. Tsar Alexander called her "the heavenly beauty." The King of Prussia cried like a child when he had to take his leave of her. He recounted this charming anecdote:

King Wilhelm met the countess as she was coming out of the church with her prayer book in her hand. "You have a beautiful prayer book, beautiful Countess," said the King. "It is at your service, Your Majesty," she answered. The king took the prayer book and leafed through it. He discovered a hand-written dedication in it: "I love you always. Love me the same. Your girlfriend N." The king wrote below this inscription: "I do what she did. I ask what she asked. Friedrich Wilhelm."

Hofbauer was the confessor of this young countess who docilely let him lead her on the path of salvation. She died at the age of only twenty-six in the presence of the saint. Five days after her death, Hofbauer wrote to Friedrich Schlosser: "Our pious Julie died like a saint...." And then he added, "If we in exile here have any cause to complain, then we should look towards our Fatherland where our tears will be dried."

With and Through the Laity

Through almost daily contact with these prominent and active personalities of the aristocracy, public life and church, Clement had his finger on the pulse of the times and thus sharpened his own sense of current issues. The saint was not only a giver but also a receiver. The Hofbauer Circle over time developed into a widely branched network of relationships among like-minded individuals. This shared attitude can be captured in a few words: Catholic and loyal to Rome.[2]

As mentioned earlier, Hofbauer's greatest concern was the further education of faithful lay apostles. His small monastery in the *Seilerstätte* was like a missionary "center." Even when Clement was in his simple apartment, he was directing missions in all of Vienna, because his friends were working in his spirit everywhere. His penitents, pupils, and followers were active in all walks of life and in all classes of society, in families, in salons, in professional and social groups, in offices, at the university, and in diplomatic circles.

Thus there was a slow, but irresistible, ever-increasing change in Vienna and beyond the borders of the city. This wave of renewal would be more than a short-lived fashion. Hofbauer looked far and wide into the future. He tried, therefore, to work broadly and deeply through the press and Christian education.

Apostolate of the Press

The saint himself was neither a poet nor a writer. He did not care much for writing, but he did care for the apostolate of the written word. Hofbauer was conscious of the great influence of the press. During his time in Warsaw, he had the works of Saint Alphonsus translated into Polish and distributed among the people. The Redemptorists even had their own small printing press at St. Benno.

In Vienna, the distribution of good books was part of his apostolate. The "Brotherhood of Mary" and the lending library that was probably founded by Diessbach and promoted by Hofbauer were supposed to fulfill this function. If Hofbauer discovered a talent for writing in one of his pupils, he encouraged him to write.

From 1814 to 1815, the *Friedensblätter* and after 1819 the *Ölzweige* were the main periodicals of the Hofbauer Circle. Clement's pupils Georg Passy, Schlegel, Werner, Veith, and others belonged to the editorial board. Much of the spirit of Hofbauer was carried into the public eye through Josef von Pilat in the official political newspaper *Der Österreichische Beobachter*, through Adam Müller in his *Staatsanzeiger*, and through Emanuel Veith in the *Balsaminen*. Friedrich Klinkowström, the painter and private tutor, edited for young people the *Wiener Sonntagsblätter*, which he illustrated himself. No less that six of Hofbauer's pupils wrote their own or translated prayer books or works of piety. Kosmaček published his *Katholisches Missionsbüchlein*, which became a religious bestseller. About four million copies were printed and distributed, and it served innumerable people as a "guide to a Christian way of life." Clement Maria Hofbauer saw the press as a kind of permanent pulpit by which people are continually influenced.

Christian Education

In Hofbauer's eyes, Christian education was the most profoundly effective pastoral work. Therefore, Clement was deeply involved in the creation of a school for the children of the aristocracy or otherwise influential parents in Vienna. In the institute, he intended to shape young people who would be reared on a sound Catholic basis. The emperor was interested in the project. During 1812, Hofbauer's friend Adam Müller worked on the realization of this plan. Religion was to be taught by Redemptorists. Thus the vicar general recalled two priests from Switzerland to Vienna. But difficulties increased. Some agitators spread a rumor that the educational institution was the work of the Jesuits. Müller was only a tool of the hated Society of Jesus. The smear campaign against the school destroyed the plan.

The plan was taken up and later realized by Friedrich Klinkowström. The saint had discovered a truly talented educator in
Klinkowström. The institute began in 1818. The existing buildings, however, were unsuitable. One day, Hofbauer and
Klinkowström were walking in the suburb of Alser. Clement
stopped in front of a large building: "This house would be perfect
for your educational institute." Friedrich responded: "We don't
have the money." And Clement: "The money will be found. Buy
it." Soon, the purchase was made and the Klinkow school was
moved there. The institute educated two hundred and ten faithful
Catholics during its sixteen years of existence; almost all of them
later took up influential positions as diplomats, officers, and so
on.

In this fashion, Hofbauer's penitents, friends, and pupils
worked as lay apostles in the most vital areas of life: in the family,
in science, in the arts and in politics. Seven of his friends would
later become bishops. Thus a deeply rooted transformation took
shape, wrought silently and without violence, as only the Spirit
can do. Cardinal Rauscher dared to speak the bold words:
"Hofbauer gave the spirit of the times a better direction." He did
this with the laity and through the laity.

CHAPTER 31

A Friend Like No Other

C lement was a saint of friendship. For him, pastoral work through human contact was writ large. He often made home visits to the poor, as well as to influential people and to scholars. For many families he was a fatherly friend. The saint was not ashamed to express feelings of friendship.

He wrote to Sophie Schlosser: "How often I wish to spend an evening in your company, beloved friend *in Christo Jesu.*" And to her husband Friedrich: "Perhaps I will be so fortunate again to spend a few joyful days in your company and embrace good Christians whom I greet heartily in friendship."

Mrs. Dorothea Schlegel wrote to a member of her family: "Old Hofbauer asks about you constantly with great love....He has a truly fatherly tenderness for us....Father Hofbauer says in his well-known manner: 'Tell him we pray for him so much that our mouths hurt.'"

A special friendship bound two very different people: Clement Maria Hofbauer and Zacharias Werner (1768–1823). Werner was a strange and willful person. As driven as he was clumsy, he was a restless man with a split personality. He is known as the founder of the fate tragedies of the German Romantic Period. The celebrated playwright was esteemed and sponsored by Goethe. In Warsaw, where Werner was a Prussian civil servant, he got to know the Bennonites. As a Freemason, Zacharias Werner hated the Redemptorists at St. Benno with a passion. His private life left a lot to be desired. He had married and divorced three times.

Apart from this, he went from one woman to the next. For years he led a desolate, wandering, and unsteady life until he came to Rome in 1809. The great hour of grace struck for him there: the Freemason and playboy Zacharias Werner became a Catholic (1810) and a priest (1814). The conversion of this man caused quite a stir, because he was known far and wide as much for his earlier frivolous life as he was for his poetry.

An Enemy Becomes a Friend

In the year of his ordination as a priest, Werner arrived in Vienna and met Hofbauer. Zacharias was caught almost immediately in the spell of the Apostle of Vienna. His carefully nourished hatred against Clement turned into friendship. In 1805 in Warsaw, Werner had written hateful things about Hofbauer and the Bennonites. "I want to become anything but Catholic....Imagine! There is an Order here: the Bennonites...who know how to tame the people because their church is open daily from seven in the morning till nine at night and they are always singing and preaching and burning incense.... Recently, I saw there (in the church) a life-size crucifix of wood and, by God, this savior did not make me a Catholic but rather a little more reasonable. Imagine a life-size, emaciated Jewish boy on the cross, stretched out, distorted, covered over and over with the most hideous and offensive wounds, a truly disgraceful caricature! Mr. War Minister, I would have

Zacharias Werner, God's trumpet.

given one hundred ducats at that moment and used them well if I had been able to break this crucifix in two across the back of this priestling!"

Later, in Vienna, it sounded radically different when Werner described Father Hofbauer as follows: "My unforgettable fatherly friend and leader, my teacher, my support, my power." In the meantime, this proud poet Zacharias Werner had entrusted himself to Hofbauer's guidance. He let himself be led like a helpless child by his father. Innumerable anecdotes illustrate this singular friendship. In 1817, Werner became deathly ill. Hofbauer took this strange old bird into his own apartment, although there was little room. He lived for almost two months "in the monastery of this religious, two small cell-like rooms where neither the sun nor the moon nor air came in." He had never lived so poorly in his life, he wrote.

In 1816, Werner had been sent to the castle of Count Janow in Poland. He was supposed to prepare the way for the eventual foundation of a Redemptorist monastery there. The poet was already quite ill at the time. Because the family of the count wanted to nurse him back to health, he remained an entire year in Janow. A strong, yet in all ways pure, and loving relationship developed between him and a young countess. Werner admitted to his confessor that he was "in love" with the count's daughter. He was convinced that Hofbauer would not allow him to travel to the castle of Janow again. But the saint was more generous and a better judge of human nature than Werner had assumed. Clement trusted his friend Zacharias a great deal. He only said to him: "I am between you both." This pastoral and pedagogical masterstroke of Hofbauer's did not miss its mark. The young countess entered a convent, and Werner's romance had a happy ending, without him or his girlfriend coming to any harm.

God's Trumpet

It was as a preacher in particular that Werner caused a great furor in Vienna. His sermons were one of the sensations during the Congress of Vienna. The crowds at his sermons were enormous. The church was full long before Mass began. The people even climbed on top of the altars and confessionals in order to find a place. The court, the aristocracy, and the simple people streamed to his sermons. One had to hear him at least once!

His reputation as a poet, his sensational conversion, his extravagant personality, his original and dramatic method of preaching, his sometimes poetic and sometimes trivial language, all this worked together to attract and carry away all those who heard him.

Before the sermon, the sacristan had to carry piles of books to the pulpit. Werner's words stirred the people. Hofbauer called him "God's trumpet." The last words of his sermons had the effect of bombs. He closed one of his sermons in the presence of many prominent guests as follows: "You undoubtedly believe that the kings and rulers have made peace? Stupidity! Amen."

Hofbauer was and remained his master and model in the preaching of the word of God. Werner repeated time and again: "He is quite original. No one outdoes him. The Holy Spirit speaks through him." The saint helped him to give up the grotesque aspects of his sermons: "Do not let yourself be ridiculed. Preach properly." Werner learned and took in much from his "friend and master." As Werner said during one sermon: "Old Hofbauer showed quite nicely at this point that we must not be discouraged, when he said: If a child falls, he will remain lying for a while, stays in the place where he has fallen, cries and screams and pounds the ground; but an adult, on the other hand, will stand up and continue on his way." This special priest was a support for Hofbauer; with his sermons he intervened powerfully in the Catholic movement.

Werner wanted to become a Redemptorist as early as 1819. He declared himself prepared to leave Austria to begin his novitiate in Switzerland. Everyone advised him against it, but Werner remained steadfast in his decision after Hofbauer's death. He began his novitiate on December 8, 1821, but abandoned it after ten months. Nevertheless Zacharias Werner kept in friendly contact with the Redemptorists until the end of his life. He named the Congregation his sole heir in his will.

CHAPTER 32

A Happy Ending

For so many years, Hofbauer dreamt of securing solid foundations and a future for his Congregation north of the Alps. As we know, his plans for new foundations failed miserably. Only two of his foundations lasted longer than three years: Warsaw and Visp. But even there Napoleon did thorough work, when he dissolved both communities overnight with a stroke of his pen.

Vicar General Hofbauer himself had to live like an exile in Vienna. He was forbidden to maintain contact with his colleagues abroad. In the Ursulines' small house, the superior of the Order lived at times with only his faithful companion Father Martin Stark. At times, Father Johannes Sabelli was there, too.[1] Their life together is described in two sentences in a handwritten report: "Our life was not rosy. But we led a familial and very religious life together."[2]

The year 1815 brought Hofbauer a new glimmer of hope. He succeeded in establishing a foundation in Walachia near Bucharest, which at the time belonged to the Turkish Empire.[3] But this foundation lasted only a short time, too.

But then, after decades of struggle, something unexpected happened. It happened as if in a detective novel—suspenseful, dramatic, and with a happy ending.

The Story Begins

Hofbauer had been a dangerous man in the eyes of the Austrian state police for a very long time. His "list of crimes" was long, and the list of his offenses grew constantly. The spies diligently went after Hofbauer's secret activities. They knew exactly with whom he associated.

In 1814, Clement committed a new crime. He secretly accepted three candidates into his community.[4] The secret service worked remarkably well. Hofbauer was summoned for questioning. He underwent extensive interrogations. Clement still had other embittered opponents in Vienna. Someone asked him if the wickedness of his enemies did not enrage him. He only showed his hands and said: "Look at my hands. They are not bloody. I have not yet spilled any blood." Actually, one should consider enemies as benefactors because they help one into heaven, he said. Priests raged against him. They wanted to remove him from their vicinity because he was a living reproach to them. The saint spoke often of "false brothers." He had his own philosophy of life in this regard: "All mischief, every scandal, comes from the clergy. We black robes are to blame for everything....A priest without the spirit of penitence is Satan's toy."

The Clever Criminal Is Not Caught

Enemies fulminated with rage and joined forces to chase the saint from the city on the Danube. The police sent a spy to the meetings of the Hofbauer Circle. But Clement saw through the evil game and spoke to his students in Latin so that the spy could not understand the most important things. The methods of Clement's opponents became still bolder. Another spy played the part of a pious man. In order to smuggle himself into Hofbauer's circle, he brought Hofbauer various Mass donations from police funds.

On another night, Clement was surrounded by his students. Two gentlemen entered and pretended to be foreign travelers. One of them played a simpleton. The other boasted constantly. Hofbauer saw through them. He said they were not foreign travelers but rather snoops sent by the secret police. These gentlemen never returned again.

Another time, someone tried to expose Clement as a Jesuit in disguise. He wore a black habit like the brothers of the Society of Jesus. Now they wanted to know what Hofbauer thought of the hated Jesuits. Hofbauer evaded the question roguishly: "The habit does not make a Jesuit," he said. "It takes a great deal to be a Jesuit." The clever saint could not be trapped. The enraged police searched further for an opportunity to catch him.

A New Capital Crime for Clement

But wait! A pretext was found, just as Clement's enemies desired. A young lady disappeared without a trace in Vienna at the end of August 1817. Hofbauer did not have the slightest thing to do with the matter. But then rumors began to circulate that the twenty-five-year-old Rosalia Brunner had been sent to a monastery abroad. The state criminal police pricked up its ears. A hot lead was discovered—Rosalia's visits to Hofbauer's house, Rosalia's desire to enter a convent, Rosalia's flight abroad. Weren't these exactly Hofbauer's well-known methods? The case of Klara Kurzmann and the case of the kidnapping of the children from Tasswitz were opened up again. The case of Rosalia Brunner was reconstructed. From unfounded assumptions came a strong suspicion and finally a "proven" fact. The file of this newest case grew ever thicker.

Finally, the matter was turned over to the courts of the church. The interrogation began negligently and spitefully: Your name? Hofbauer! Your first name? Clement Maria! Your religion? Hofbauer became impatient with the bureaucratic red tape. He answered irritably: "It is generally well-known that I am a Catholic priest." The accused got a sharp rebuke for this remark. Then the priest lost his patience: "It is no good being here," he said. And the delinquent immediately disappeared from the courtroom. The judges looked at one another puzzled. The session was over.

An Attack in Clement's Own House

A new scene is now added to this story in 1818. Hofbauer's secretary, Father Sabelli, is the cause. This intelligent, multilingual man had always had little regard for the vicar general. Perhaps Hofbauer was also to blame for certain tensions. Nevertheless, one day Father Sabelli decided to leave Vienna. From the superior general in Rome, he surreptitiously obtained a transfer to another

country. Hofbauer was faced with a *fait accompli*. This action
hurt the saint deeply and he spent many sleepless nights.

Sabelli had to obtain a pass. He told the authorities that he had
to travel on business for the Order. The civil servants' ears pricked
up. So, Hofbauer was a member of an Order whose leadership was
abroad. That would be incriminating enough to deport Clement.

On November 12, 1818, a three-man commission suddenly
appeared at the apartment of the Redemptorists. Dr. Madlener
who was staying with Hofbauer at the time was sent out, and the
doors were barricaded. All the drawers, all the books and papers,
every corner of the house, were expertly searched. Then a punc-
tilious, three-hour interrogation followed.

The agents were disappointed. They had not found the expected evidence. Now they applied pressure on Hofbauer. By ap-
plying the law from 1781 that forbade Austrian members of a
religious order from maintaining contact with foreign monasteries and superiors abroad, Hofbauer was given a choice: either to
resign from the Redemptorist Congregation or to leave the country. The saint did not hesitate. Better to accept the fate of banish-
ment once again than be unfaithful to his calling. He dared make
only one request. Because he was old, he asked not to be banned
from Austria in the middle of the hard winter. Everything was
taken down in the minutes.

The search was over and the agents wanted to leave. Hofbauer
asked: "Are we done?" The officials said they were. Clement, however, pointed to heaven in a warning gesture: "One thing remains—
Judgment Day."

After this inquisitorial raid, a friend came to visit. He heard
Hofbauer singing one of his favorite songs: "O Heaven, hear my
pleas."

Short-Legged Lies

The emperor was presented with a report—a lie—that Hofbauer
had himself expressed the desire to leave Austria. The good monarch said: "Now, if Father Hofbauer himself wants to go, I have
nothing against it. But since he is a native son, I would not have
sent him away." The false document was approved by the em-

peror on December 26. This was a strange present on Hofbauer's sixty-eighth birthday! The experiences of the last weeks had disheartened the old saint. He was wounded, downcast, and discouraged. His decision was firm, he would leave Vienna in May.

On January 28, 1819, Hofbauer wrote the bishop a letter. He would obey the sovereign's order and emigrate. He did not leave Austria of his own free will but rather by necessity. Thus the fraud was uncovered. Archbishop Hohenwart wrote the emperor without delay; he described the true facts to him and confessed: "I am losing my best priest." Now our saint's friends intervened. As early as February 7, the monarch ordered an inquiry into this affair by the imperial chancery and demanded complete disclosure.[5] Hofbauer's enemies began to feel the heat. They tried to worm their way out of their uncomfortable position through misrepresentations. They passed the buck from one to the other. In vain! The shameful game of intrigue had been exposed.

A Happy Ending

Just at this time, the emperor traveled to Italy, and he also visited the pope. Pius VII knew Hofbauer personally. During the audience, he congratulated the Austrian monarch: he had a truly apostolic priest in Father Hofbauer. He elegantly mentioned in an aside that Clement was not at all pleased with the Romans. The emperor pricked up his ears. What, Hofbauer was not pleased with the curia in Rome? Then he was not at all this inveterate "Papist" and "Roman" that he had been taken for at court.

From Rome, the emperor traveled to Naples, the homeland of Saint Alphonsus, the cradle of the Redemptorist Congregation. Emperor Franz asked about this religious community. He also studied the stack of files that the imperial chancery had sent him regarding the case against Hofbauer. It was now clear to the Emperor that Hofbauer had been treated very unjustly. On May 23, he decreed that Hofbauer should remain in Vienna and present the statutes of his Order. That was the great turning point.

The emperor was in Vienna again in August. Hofbauer was granted an audience with him and requested approval for his Order in Austria. There was also talk of the church of Maria-am-Gestade becoming the Redemptorists' primary responsibility.

The die had been cast. Approval of the Redemptorists in Austria and the transfer of the church of Maria-am-Gestade was now only a matter of time. Hofbauer worked at a feverish pace over the next few weeks. With the help of his friends, he brought the statutes of the Order of the Redemptorists into harmony with the current laws. As early as October 29, 1819, he was able to present the emperor with the rewritten statutes, accompanied by a letter.

These were days of waiting, long days of drama, and tension! Then one day Baron Penkler burst into Hofbauer's house. He was so agitated he could barely speak. He embraced his friend Clement and managed only to utter the words: "Let a *Te Deum* be sung. Father Hofbauer, we have won." And Hofbauer rejoiced. He had finally seen his life's dream realized.

Someone gave the old vicar general several packages of sugar and coffee. Hofbauer zealously laid them in a reserve for the monastic community which was to be founded. "This will all be for our confreres at Maria Stiegen." Symbolic gestures of a caring, fatherly man!

The imperial decree for the approval of the Congregation was ready to be signed in March. Then death struck.

CHAPTER 33

The Great Pilgrim
at His Goal

In the spring of 1819, Father Hofbauer was so ill that every one feared the worst. But once again he recovered. The Sisters at the convent of St. Ursula rejoiced at his recovery. He only joked: "You are fine friends! You won't even grant me heaven."

The following winter was hard. In biting cold and wading through snow, the old priest made his way as usual every morning at four o'clock to the faraway Viennese suburb, to the church of the Capuchins on the *Platzl*. Then the year 1820 began. Father Martin Stark, who lived in the upper floor of the same house, fell ill in February. Father Hofbauer had to take care of him. The saint climbed the stairs with great difficulty. Once he said to his colleague: "Martin, I don't know which of us is sicker." And in fact, Clement was very ill. On the path from his apartment to the convent of the Ursulines across the street, one could often see the trail of blood that Hofbauer had left behind.

On March 5, the Third Sunday of Lent, Father Hofbauer gave his last sermon in the church of St. Ursula. On the following Wednesday he heard the confessions of the sisters for the last time— standing. He could not sit for the pain. He left the convent faster than usual this time. To one sister he said: "Pray for me, I am very sick." The dismayed nun answered: "It would be a terrible misfortune for us, if we were to lose you." And he smiled: "Only sin is a misfortune." On Thursday, a Mass was said in the Minorite Church for the deceased Princess Thekla Jablonovska. This noble lady had been one of the greatest benefactors of the Bennonites in Warsaw. After she died in Rome on February 14, 1820, her relatives in Vienna asked Father Hofbauer to say a memorial Mass for the deceased on March 9. This Thursday was a cold day, and it was snowing. Clement Hofbauer sang the Requiem. Madlener and Pajalich assisted him as deacon and subdeacon. Toward the end of the Mass, Clement became quite pale. They were afraid he would faint. After the Mass, Baron Penkler had the deathly ill man driven home in the baron's carriage.

Eternal Peace

Now events pressed upon one another. Hofbauer's friend and physician Dr. Emanuel Veith hurried to the sickbed. There was little hope left. From time to time, Hofbauer whispered his favorite prayer: "What God wants, as God wants and when God wants." The maid at the convent brought the sick man some food. When Marianne saw the saint lying there in such suffering, she cried bitterly. Clement, who was her confessor, comforted her: "Marianne, do not cry. Soon you will also be with me." And in fact, the loyal maid would follow him into eternity a few days later.

Then they sent for Clement's confessor, Father Schmid. Clement confessed his sins and received the last rites. At one time, Madlener was alone at the bed of Hofbauer. Clement grabbed the hand of his friend and pupil: "Dear Madlener, great secrets are going to the grave with me. I would gladly entrust you with them but you can't keep quiet."

Dr. Johann Emanuel Veith (1787–1876). Hofbauer's friend and physician. Later, he became one of the most famous preachers of Austria.

Hofbauer remained silent. Madlener would later say: "Hofbauer was like a sealed book during his last hours."

Dr. Veith spent the entire night at the bed of his friend. The dying man had a peaceful night. He spoke not a word. Only the noise of his death rattle was heard.

March 15 was to be the day of the saint's death. At six in the morning Clement opened his eyes. He smiled in a friendly manner, like a child. With a broken voice he prayed the beginning of his favorite prayers: "Everything for the glory of my God." Midday came. Dr. Veith and the confessor, Franz Schmid, the two young theologians, Madlener and Pajalich, Professor Zängerle and the maid of the convent, Marianne, were standing around the bed of the dying man. It was noon. The bells rang for prayers. Hofbauer gathered his remaining strength and said: "Pray, they are ringing the *Angelus*." Those were his last words. Everyone knelt down and prayed. When they stood up, Clement was dead. Like his beloved father in the Congregation, Alphonsus Liguori, Father Clement Maria Hofbauer peacefully went into the presence of God at the ringing of the *Angelus*. The tireless pilgrim reached the goal of his wandering after all his struggles. Consternation was great. "Everyone is deeply moved." As he often had to live, so the saint died: not in a monastery but in a strange house, separated from his colleagues whom he loved so much.

Gradually, those present recovered from the shock. They dressed the deceased in the habit of the Congregation. As a symbol of his priestly dignity and his missionary work, they wrapped a beautiful stole around him. The tools of suffering of the Savior and the image of the suffering mother were embroidered on the stole. After the corpse had been laid out in the apartment, large candles were lit and placed on candlesticks.

The official formalities were seen to: the preparation of the death certificate and the sealing of the property. But the official did not have much work to do. The furniture belonged to the Ursulines. Only a few articles of clothing, books, personal objects, and some packets of sugar that the saint had saved for his young confreres at Maria-am-Gestade were left. That was the sum of his wealth.

The Power of Helplessness

The news of Hofbauer's death spread through Vienna like wildfire. The Ursuline nuns were just going down to lunch when they heard the sad news. All of them cried out and sobbed. Instead of going to the dining hall, they went to church. Father Martin Stark was ill. The news of Hofbauer's death so overwhelmed him that he lost his head. Only from his bed could he give a few instructions.

The dead man lay there peacefully, smiling benevolently, as if he were asleep. There was no trace of deathly pallor in his face. And now a great migration of people began. His friends and penitents came from far and wide. All the witnesses agreed: the room was usually crammed full, the crowd was so large. Most of the people were crying. Touching scenes took place. Many kissed the cold hands of the dead man. One had to prevent the sobbing Countess Széchényi from kissing the corpse because the danger of infection was too great. The noble lady said simply, "Saints do not infect." The friends of the saint consoled one another, "Now we have an intercessor in heaven." Everyone wanted to get a souvenir of Clement. Some cut hair from the head of the dead man, others cut off pieces of his habit, still others tried to touch the corpse with objects they had brought with them. Finally, guards were posted in order to protect the house and the body from these plunderers.

That evening, Chaplain Rinn came and drew the face of the deceased. Beneath the portrait the artist wrote this biblically influenced phrase: "Blessed the eyes which saw you and were distinguished by your friendship."

Love Prepares Everything

Apparently, no one saw to Hofbauer's burial. Only the time and place of the funeral service and the burial were determined. The funeral service was to be in St. Stephen's Cathedral on the evening of March 16, and burial the following day in the cemetery of Maria-Enzersdorf. Everything else was left to chance. Father Stark, who was the only Redemptorist in Vienna at the time, ordered from his sickbed that Vicar General Hofbauer was to be buried quietly without any great ceremonies. That may have been the right way: the deceased was not counted among the great in this world, but rather among the poorest of the poor of Vienna.

Everything changed in the course of the afternoon. What happened seems like a fairy tale. First, an expensive coffin was brought into the house. It was donated—it was said. Then a few small groups of people gathered in front of the house. Their numbers grew and grew and grew. Prominent people were driven to Johannes Alley in coaches. Students, seminarians, priests, and professors arrived.

The funeral procession began in late afternoon. Twelve young people carried the coffin. Still more people gathered together from all the side streets and alleys. Here is a representative statement of an eyewitness: "Thousands gathered together from the city and far-away suburbs without invitation. The poor were very numerous...and mourned the death of their confessor and benefactor with loud sobbing."

Then it grew dark. And again something strange happened.

The cemetery of the Romantics in Maria-Enzersdorf. First burial place of St. Clement (between the family of Friedrich von Klinkowström and the spouses Adam and Sophie Müller).

Candles were suddenly distributed. No one knew who had donated them. Suddenly everything was transformed into a sea of light.

As if this were not strange enough! The so-called "Great Gate" of St. Stephen's Cathedral is opened very rarely, on extraordinary occasions and only then for the most prominent personalities. To the bewilderment of everyone, the main doors opened. No one ever found out who had arranged this unusual honor. "Love had prepared everything."

Soon the cathedral was full to the last seat. The cathedral could not hold everyone. The theology students of the archbishop's seminary were present in full strength at the funeral Mass. Later the angered director of the seminary wanted to know who had granted permission or who had ordered their attendance. No one knew the answer. The theology students said that the word was spread throughout the seminary that everyone should take part in the celebration.

The funeral Mass began. Zacharias Werner sang the prescribed chants. His voice quivered with emotion. Dorothea Schlegel described the inspiration of this hour to her friend Sophie Schlosser: "All the altars in St. Stephen's were covered with burning candles: a crowd of school children sang such beautiful songs that I believed I heard the angels singing." After the celebration, the corpse was carried into the crypt.

On the following day, the burial took place among Hofbauer's closest friends at the cemetery of Maria-Enzersdorf near Mödling. Hofbauer himself had expressed the wish to be buried there. This cemetery was the burial place of the Penkler family. Furthermore, Hofbauer's great model, Father Diessbach of the Society of Jesus, had been buried there in 1798.

A Real Triumph

Thus, after his death, Hofbauer's body was carried as if in triumphant through the streets of the very city in which he had earlier suffered so many humiliations. "Yes, this is how God rewards his zealous and faithful servants even before the eyes of their enemies." All the reports agree: the burial of this poor Redemptorist priest was one of the greatest that Vienna had ever seen—a truly triumphant procession. The papal nuncio wrote: "It appears God wanted to compensate him with this triumph for all the persecutions he had to suffer in his life."

Friedrich Schlegel expressed what many other friends and pupils of Hofbauer also felt: "Here a great and holy man has gone and I see only a great void before me." The emperor, several papal nuncios, bishops, and the superior general of the Redemptorists praised the achievements of the deceased.

A hymn of praise to the deceased appeared in the newspaper the *Österreichischer Beobachter* the day after the funeral: "The walls of St. Benno in Warsaw would attest to what one single true servant of God like this man could achieve under the most unfavorable conditions and in the most difficult situations, if thousands of living witnesses were not present whom he had fed, clothed and led back to God and a Christian way of life…. Posterity will harvest the fruits of his rich and truly apostolic life among us."

Hofbauer commemorative stamp.

CHAPTER 34

The Saint Among Us: An Interpretation

I cannot completely understand a person; I interpret him. Thus the attempt to interpret the life, the achievements, and the personality of another is always a risk. This hazardous venture would not be permissible if I were to presume to make a final judgment of a person (even of a saint). An attempt at an interpretation, however, also appears to be a responsible Christian act as long as I simply strive respectfully to perceive the "true" person.

We can imagine the person of Clement Hofbauer in a blurred form through the many statements of his friends and penitents, and through the numerous reports of the police and his enemies. Let's call it an outline.

Clement Maria Hofbauer: A Sketch

Clement was of average height and stocky build with broad shoulders, a short neck, and powerful chest. His head was bent slightly forward, was rather round and Slavic. He had black-brown hair that was flecked with gray in old age. There was a wonderful calm over his lively facial features. His mouth usually bore a smile betraying a jovial, benevolent person. The saint's small eyes were usually half closed. One could hardly resist his sharp, fiery look. His lisping voice and delicate hands stood in contrast to his powerful figure. All in all, a precious mixture of power and tenderness.

At first glance, Clement appeared to be a man of energy, of perseverance, a kind person full of love and tenderness who was capable of great friendships.

As for his character, Hofbauer was always described by his contemporaries as an extremely honest and forthright man. He was a stranger to everything related to deception, slyness, dishonesty, and boastfulness. He often said openly and bluntly what he thought. He could also criticize sharply. He abhorred power struggles and party politics. In his relationships with others, he was very humane, uncomplicated, and simple. He was, it seems, a very practical man who never shied away from kitchen chores or working in the fields, even as a priest and as a vicar general.

The following traits were blended together in this man as if in a mold: the practical craftsman and the missionary filled with the Holy Spirit, the hermit and the wandering apostle, the friend to the poor and the dinner companion of the aristocracy, deep warmth and active work, the love of this world and the longing for the next.

The Enemy Within

Behind Hofbauer's robust peasant nature lay a good heart that could give itself selflessly beyond belief. But we must finally stop presenting the saints as perfect supermen or as virtuosos of virtue high above us in every respect. Clement Maria Hofbauer also carried an enemy in his own breast. By nature, he was very lively and impetuous, irritable and easily angered. There is no doubt that his colleagues sometimes had to suffer under his irascible nature. But whenever he noticed that his temper had run away with him, he could tap his chest contritely and say: "I am a scoundrel."

The saint once snapped at a colleague very harshly. The man was hurt and left the room of the superior. But it did not take long for Clement to appear with a sheet of music in his hand. He called to the colleague he had just insulted and said to him: "Do you know this song? Come, sing it with me."

Another amusing event makes us smile. It took place in

Hofbauer's apartment in Vienna. At the time, two younger colleagues were living with him there. Clement got along well with Martin Stark. But there had often been tensions between him and Johannes Sabelli. As can often happen, even among members of the same community, a bitter quarrel broke out between the superior and the young subordinate. Hofbauer exploded, "Just do whatever you want! I have had it with staying with both of you. I am going to America." And indeed he packed his bag and disappeared without saying good-bye. As he marched through the city, his anger receded. Lost in thought, he arrived at the Church of Mariahilf (Help of Mary) and went in. He was overcome with bitter remorse. He realized the stupid situation he had put himself in. Return? Impossible! As superior—this would be humiliating! What would his colleagues say? "Converted all of America already?" No, he could not afford that. He took refuge in Mary and prayed approximately as follows: "You have helped many in their distress. Today, you must free me from my dilemma. The ideal solution would be for my colleagues to come here and ask me to return home." The poor man prayed for a long time but the two young Redemptorists did not come to bring him home. Finally, Clement left the church and slowly headed for Upper Austria while praying the rosary. Suddenly, he heard loud panting behind him. He turned around. His two repentant brothers were standing there out of breath. They asked him for forgiveness and pleaded with him to return home. We can imag-

St. Clement Maria Hofbauer (1751–1820).

ine the rest ourselves. Saint Clement would surely allow us the question: Who had earned the right to be canonized on that day, "Old Hofbauer" or his young companions?

A Poor Old Fool

Although Father Hofbauer himself suffered from his explosive temperament, he had to learn to live with conflicts. But Clement did not break down under the weight of his own imperfections. With a dose of self-irony, he encouraged himself: "Every day I thank God that he left me my high spirits and my irritability, because they keep me humble and prevent me from becoming proud." A saint who accepts his faults without raging against himself, a flawed saint who has enough humor to call himself "an old donkey" and an "old fool," is also preaching the Gospel for the people of today. We feel close to this saint.

Rooted in God

"The saints are lived Gospel," says Alphonsus Liguori. We could also call a holy person in this sense an image of God, a living statement of God, and a living reference to God. Somehow God places the saint among us now.

But every icon reveals and conceals at the same time. God is always so completely different, unfathomable, and eternal. Perhaps for that reason the saints transcend time and place, are not bound to any place or any century. After their death, their message continues into the future. For this reason, every generation must discover anew what a saint has to say to it even as a historical model.

A Man of Faith

Clement Hofbauer was, as far as his faith is concerned, a phenomenon. He was so taken and filled with God that faith appeared to be something he took for granted. His faith was at once innate and incarnate in him so that his entire life was a life lived from faith. Clement himself admitted that he could not expect any reward in this regard because he believed without hindrance;

yes, he would even have to force himself to doubt. He could point with his finger to a visible object and say he doubted the existence of God less than the presence of that thing. He had difficulty understanding how people could live without faith. A person without faith was like a fish out of water. Human beings were created in the image of God to such an extent that there were probably no genuine atheists. He would say sarcastically, "Imagine everything that non-believers must believe in order not to be believers."

Faith for Hofbauer was not first and foremost a rational understanding of the Christian articles of faith, but rather a surrendering to God, a friendly connection to the person of the Savior. His joy in and from his faith came from this understanding. Faith for him was anything but a duty or a must. Time and again he spoke of the great privilege in being allowed to believe. He thanked God for this gift and said it would be better to lose one's life than to let the faith decline. One of his prayers begins with the words: "Take everything, but not the valuable treasure of faith." Clement knew that his deep faith was a blessing, an undeserved gift. He asserted often with gratitude that he would never exchange his faith for that of another.

He insisted on making the strangest statements. If someone said to him that God could be seen with one's own eyes at a certain place, he would close his eyes and say: "My faith does not need any such proof."

It was surely the integrity of his rock-solid faith that made such a deep impression on everyone. One witness at the process of canonization summarized all this in one sentence: "His faith was a living faith; he related everything to God."

On a First-Name Basis With God

Clement Hofbauer was never a sanctimonious man, but rather a "man of faith and prayer." Because the heart of his faith lay in an intimate friendship with God, his life was a trusting relationship with God.

As a former hermit, Hofbauer was always looking within. A confidant of Hofbauer's gives us a glimpse into the depths of this very active man's life of faith:

Father Hofbauer led a very active life in Vienna....He had only one room which was open to all....There he created in his heart a desert, a lonely cell, a small oratory. Into this loneliness of the heart...he would withdraw whenever he wanted to, at any time, wherever he found himself, even when he wandered through the most crowded streets, he immersed himself in himself.

Father Srna knew Clement well, because for years he lived with him in very close quarters. He claimed that Hofbauer was a great man of prayer "because prayer was the nourishment and refreshment of his heart."

Wherever the saint arrived, he enthusiastically promoted liturgical prayer. The Eucharist formed a central point in his faith life. All the witnesses spoke of the emotion with which he celebrated the Eucharist or carried the monstrance with the Blessed Sacrament "as if the presence of the Savior held him captive." He could spend a long time before the tabernacle and engage in intimate dialogues with Christ as one friend would with another.

One does not need to mention that he also felt an inner devotion to the Mother of Our Lord. Hofbauer was a great devotee of Mary. For that reason, he wrote in a letter that he preferred it whenever one added the name Mary to his name of Clement.

A Man of Hope

If God is infinite love, then he wants our best. Accordingly, the answer given by human beings can only be: hoping and trusting, fulfilling the will of God and seeking his glory. Clement repeats this thought constantly. From his mouth, these are not merely so-called pious sayings. The entire life of this man tested by suffering is proof enough of this. His pithy sayings summarize entire books; they do not need any explanation.

- The love of God be your motivation, the will of God your guiding-principle, the glory of God your goal.

- What God wants, as God wants, when God wants.

- Not as I wish but rather as God wills.

- Everything for the glory of God.

- Jesus, I want to live as long as You will; I want to suffer as You will me to; I want to die as soon as You will it.

- The union of your will with the divine will is more pleasing to God than fasting and other mortifications of the flesh.

- The best means for becoming holy is to sink one's self into the divine will like a stone into the sea and to let one's self be rolled around and thrown at will.

- Let us place all our trust in God. One must hope against hope because what appears impossible to man is possible for God.

During his entire life, until his final illness, Clement sang his favorite song every morning: "Everything for the glory of my God, to increase the praise and honor of God, at work and at rest."

A Kindly Saint

Clement Maria Hofbauer was not a melancholy person despite his many failures and the constant persecutions directed against him, but rather a joyful saint. One never saw him moody or embittered; he called sadness "vapors from hell." He even possessed a goodly portion of humor and was not averse to a harmless joke. He lived and preached patience, holy unconcern, and the light-hearted joy of the children of God. He hated the Jansenists who poisoned the joy of the faithful in the name of religion.

This saint with the charisma of humanity frowned upon everything that was extravagant. He was strict with himself but not unmerciful. In his old age, in contrast with his younger years, he permitted himself a good glass of wine or a cup of coffee. Then he praised wine as a valuable gift of God, especially for fortifying one's strength in old age.

When directing penitents he also let reason prevail. He was of the opinion that in regard to religious matters the usual paths were the surest. Inner mortification was more important than terrible lacerations of the flesh. "It is good and wholesome to undergo a brief mortification from time to time, but this must only happen occasionally without compulsion or anxiety." He also recommended time and again prayer and reflection on the suffering of Christ. "But one must do it gently, without strain, just as one thinks of a friend or a green field." Such talk does us good. We feel some connection to a reasonable, humane saint.

An Apostolic Man

Clement Hofbauer was a Redemptorist, a missionary through and through. Sophie Schlosser expressed this essential element of his life when she wrote of him: "During his sermons I often imagine that the Apostles must have spoken like this." In reading the documents about him, one notices how often he is characterized by his contemporaries as a "truly apostolic man." "His entire appearance was something that drew one to God."

Hofbauer tried to realize the Redemptorist ideal. It was important to him to become a missionary according to his calling and his mandate. He feared only one thing—disloyalty. For that reason, he never simply raged in a senseless, hectic manner. As a missionary and Redemptorist, he took a stand against a turbulent era in world history. He had the courage to recognize the will and calling of God in the concrete events and situations of the day. He had the strength not to waste any time but rather to seize the moment for God. He was free enough to adapt his apostolic methods because he knew he was a modest tool in the hands of the Savior, like a broom the master uses and then stands in the corner. Thus he was never intoxicated by his successes, and he remained calm and available for further challenges in the face of thousands of failures and persecutions. The apostolic man knew that God is here in history—"With him is plentiful Redemption" (Psalm130:7, which was taken as the motto for the coat of arms of the Congregation of the Redemptorists).

The Redemptorist church Maria-am-Gestade in Vienna.

Epilogue

Posterity Will Reap
the Harvest

CHAPTER 35

The Triumph

An earthly biography ends with the death of a person. But there are those who have died who shape the present and future more than some of the living. Clement Maria Hofbauer can be counted among these people. He even appears to be more important in death than he was in life. "Posterity will reap the harvest of his truly apostolic life among us."

Hofbauer's funeral was a great triumph. His final resting place, the cemetery of Maria-Enzersdorf soon became a kind of shrine. Innumerable people visited his grave. They were convinced that this man who had helped them so much on earth could also be their intercessor in heaven.

Many of his penitents and friends wished to be buried close to Hofbauer's grave: Josef von Pilat and his wife, Friedrich von Klinkowström and his wife, Baron Penkler, Adam Müller, Zacharias Werner, and others. This place is called the Cemetery of the Romantics because various members of the circle of Romantics who gathered around Hofbauer are buried there.

On November 4, 1862, Hofbauer's last remains were brought in a rather triumphant procession to the Redemptorist Church of Maria-am-Gestade in Vienna. Once, in a completely desperate, hopeless situation, he had written: "God knows where my old bones will rest until the resurrection." At the time, he could hardly have imagined that a reliquary in the church of Maria-am-Gestade would one day contain his bones.

In 1888, Pope Leo XIII proclaimed Clement Maria Hofbauer

venerable. In 1909, Pius X declared Clement a saint and made him the patron saint of Vienna in 1914.

Clement's greatest success began after his death.

Saint Clement Maria Hofbauer's funeral monument in the church of Maria-am-Gestade in Vienna (sculptor Gassner).

CHAPTER 36

Hofbauer's Dream Becomes Reality

Hofbauer's life's wish to establish the Congregation of the Redemptorists north of the Alps has been mentioned often in this book. For over three decades, he doggedly worked in vain for the realization of this dream. The saint prayerfully placed his plans in the hands of God. Gradually, the unmistakable feeling grew in him that the Congregation of the Redemptorists would only be permitted in Austria after his death. His prophecy was fulfilled by God's loyal punctuality.

Some witnesses want to claim that the emperor signed the decree permitting the foundation on the day the saint died. It is historically proven that the imperial decree officially allowing the Congregation in Austria appeared exactly five weeks after Hofbauer's death. The content of the document is clear: the Congregation of the Redemptorists is to be established in Vienna, the upper Passau building was to be its first monastery, and the bordering church, Maria-am-Gestade, was to be the Redemptorists' church.[1] Before the church and house were turned over to the Redemptorists, they were to be renovated at the cost of the state.

Those pupils of Hofbauer who planned to enter the new community met for a discussion. A dozen of them were prepared to begin the novitiate immediately. Others announced that they would have to wait a while for the realization of their intention. Since the renovations in the Passau building would take some time, thirty-two candidates addressed a request to the emperor. They asked the monarch for permission to begin their novitiate without delay in another house. Their request was granted.

As early as May 19, the first candidates entered their provisional novitiate house and began their novitiate year on August 1. Zacharias Werner gave the sermon. The young religious community took possession of its new house at Maria-am-Gestade[2] before Christmas and celebrated the first solemn High Mass on Christmas day in this splendid Gothic church.

The new community grew very quickly. In April 1821, there were already twenty-seven candidates at the monastery of Maria-am-Gestade.[3] One year later, the number of members had risen to forty-nine. The seed that Clement had sown with difficulty and tears took root. Hofbauer's dream, too, of being able to send missionaries to other countries has been realized. Thus the saint was the great pioneer for the spread of the Redemptorist Congregation in the whole world.

These two saints of the Congregation never met each other personally. But without Saint Alphonsus, the founder of the Redemptorist Congregation, a Saint Clement Hofbauer would not have been thinkable.

CHAPTER 37

Hofbauer and the Reform Movement in the Church

Clement Maria Hofbauer was a man of his times. His concept of the Church and the ecumenical movement obviously do not correspond exactly with what we conceive
the Church to be today.

The saint viewed the Church of Jesus Christ as his mother and
as the family of God's children here on earth. He loved it with a
childlike love. He often repeated one of his pithy sayings: "How
can someone have God as a father, if he does not want to have the
Church as a mother." The missionary Hofbauer went very far in
his zeal; he would have liked to convert all the people of the world
to Christ and lead them to unity of faith, "so that they will become one flock with one shepherd" (John 10:16). "If only I could
have the grace to convert all the mis-believers and non-believers! I
would carry them into the holy Catholic Church in my arms and
on my shoulders." Many men and women of other denomina-
tions and other religions found their way to the Catholic Church
through Hofbauer. This conversion movement also took hold of
famous people in the sciences, arts, and politics. But Clement
Hofbauer was not an intolerant fanatic who was only concerned
with gaining as many converts as possible. For his time, he even
showed an amazing amount of ecumenical spirit.[1]

"I believe in the one, holy, Catholic Church"—Clement
Hofbauer often preached this article of the creed. He often ex-

189

plained these words of Christ: "Father, let them all be one so that the world may believe" (John 17:21).

Hofbauer saw the sign and guarantee of unity in the Bishop of Rome. Rome was not just the destination of his pilgrimages. The pope lived in this city. And it was the pope who stood at the root of his joy in the pilgrimage, because Clement's "faith was so strong, his love of the Church, and his reverence and submission to the visible leader of the Church was great."

But Hofbauer was born into a time that was turning against the Church, Rome, and the pope himself. The pope was imprisoned and kidnapped by Napoleon. State-churchism and the away-from-Rome movement flourished. The saint feared for the Church he loved.

He tried to work for the unity and reform of the Church through the papal nuncios. Clement enjoyed their complete confidence and enjoyed friendly relationships with the Nuncios of Warsaw, Saluzzo (1784–1794), and Litta (1794–1795), as well as with those of Vienna, Severoli (1801–1817), and Leardi (1817–1823). His greatest friends were also men who were all strict Catholics and loyal to Rome, such as Diessbach, Penkler, Beroldinger, Franz Schmid, and others.[2]

Hofbauer was denounced as unreasonably loyal to Rome and as an obsequious Papist. Although he was loyal to Rome, he had dared nonetheless to level criticism, even bitter criticism, against the Roman curia.[3] More than any other person, a saint who loved the Catholic Church and the pope so much, who was so concerned with the unity of the Church, could permit himself some constructive criticisms.

Church Politics Under Fire

Nothing would be more mistaken than to see Hofbauer as a church diplomat or a bureaucrat. No, the saint was first and foremost a pastor and a missionary. Obviously, pastoral activity is, however, always also something of political activity on behalf of the Church. When the emperor and kings, princes and diplomats, came to the city on the Danube for the Congress of Vienna at the end of September 1814, Hofbauer reached the zenith of his involvement in church politics. The saint himself did not take part in these proceedings and, yet, he was somehow there, in the background. The Congress dealt with, among other things, the reorganization of the German church. Influential people sought advice from Father Hofbauer. His reputation in Catholic circles was so great that he was even seen as a candidate for bishop. To the great consternation of the saint, the Congress broke up without coming to any decision regarding longstanding Church issues.

Before and during the Congress of Vienna, Hofbauer's loyalty to the Church and his own organizational politics brought him into conflict with other men interested in reform. Clement Hofbauer, Ignatius Wessenberg, and Michael Sailer were typical representatives of three movements within the German Catholic Reform Movement at the beginning of the nineteenth century. The spiritual positions of these three men were so different, however, that there were bitter disputes between them.

Wessenberg fought for a German National Church with a German leader independent of Rome. Hofbauer saw in this plan an attack against the unity of the Church and the threat of a schism. He tried to stop this partition of the Church with all the means at his disposal.

Johann Michael Sailer (1751–1832) was without doubt an important man in the Church and a very controversial person. Mysticism had influenced him in a special way. While he was devoted to the reform of the Church, his starting point differed essentially from that of Hofbauer. Sailer emphasized a mystical concept of the Church and tolerance between the various confessions. Hofbauer reproached the former professor for not being Catholic enough and accused him of blurring the lines between the various confessions; he taught only an inner Christianity and rejected the external forms (for example, sacraments and worship).[4] Hofbauer's assessment of Sailer is simply unfair in many aspects. Even the saints are people with limits. In Saint Clement Maria's life, this attitude to Sailer is surely a black mark. False information, suspicion and prejudice, another view of the Church, and different approaches to the renewal of the Church were surely the causes of this unpleasant conflict.

Clement Maria Hofbauer was concerned first and foremost

with the renewal of the faith, and the unity and reform of the Church from within. He saw the greatest danger for the Church in the simplification of the faith. It was clear to him that a real reform of the Church had always to be first a path inward, a path back to the middle, and into the deep. Thus, he began his attempts at renewal in the confessional, at the altar, in the pulpit, on his knees, and in discussions of the faith.

After his death, Clement's many lay followers, people whom Clement had educated, continued to work in his spirit. They became bearers of a Catholic Reform Movement that influenced an entire era in the German-speaking countries. Hofbauer's will to shape the future through faith was worthwhile. "Austria again became Catholic through this dead man."

Let us end this book with a prayer of Saint Clement Maria Hofbauer:

Oh Father of mercy, look into the face of your anointed one, who pleads for his bride and our mother, the holy Church, with a loud voice and tears. See, oh my Father, the bloody sweat, the terrible crown of thorns, the hands and feet that have been pierced by nails, the wounds of our brother Jesus Christ: hear, oh Father, the sobs of your much beloved Son on the cross. They have moved the heavens, split the rocks. Should your mercy remain unmoved? Keep everyone who recognizes you with an sincere heart within the holy faith, protect everyone from false prophets who go about in sheep's clothing but are ferocious wolves on the inside; keep their power away so that their attacks may fail and they be destroyed. Merciful God, grant to those who believe in you the grace to love you continually in unity and love, to follow you loyally into death and there to praise and honor you for ever.

Illustrations

Studio R, Redemptorists, Munich: p. 5, 7, 9, 12, 14, 21, 23, 28, 46, 73, 83, 84, 88, 92, 103, 104, 105, 109, 111, 113, 114, 128, 148, 149, 157, 167, 172, 175, 181, 186, 188.

Brother Karl Elsasser, C.Ss.R.: p. 76, 141, 170.

For the most part, the maps were compiled by Father Brudzisz, C.Ss.R.: p. 40, 78, 86, 94.

Notes

PREFACE

1. Father Ladislaus Szoldrski collected and published a great many documents in the fifteen volumes of the *Monumenta Hofbaueriana*, Cracow, Torun, Rome 1915–1951. The following notes without additional information refer to this collection: the Roman numerals refer to the volume numbers I–XV and the Arabic numbers to the page numbers of each volume. *Spicilegium Historicum Congregationis SSmi Redemptoris, Collegium S. Alfonsi de Urbe* (beginning 1953). Subsequently referred to as *SH* (Roman numerals = volume, Arabic = page number). I have used the various articles on St. Clement Hofbauer which have appeared in *SH*: II (1954) 152–190, 432–465, III 412–446, IV 87–112, 113–120, V 335–405, 415–421, VI 484–485, VII, VIII 69–127, IX 129–202, XII 214–218, XV 145–147, XVII 225–253, XVIII, XX 24–44, 386–392, XXIII 476, XXVII 275–277, XVIII 213–223, XXXII 153–184. Readers interested in fuller documentation and references may consult the original German edition published by Kanisius Verlag as *Das Evangelium neu verkünden: Klemens Maria Hofbauer* (Freiburg 1987).

CHAPTER 3

1. XIII 329, XI 324, 317. Hofbauer's first pilgrimage to Rome most likely took place in 1768–1769. His traveling companion was Emmanuel (Peter) Kunzmann (VIII 146). Hofbauer's last pilgrimage to Rome was in 1803 (III 91, XI 175, 278).
2. XII 234. According to this report, Thaddeus Hübl and Emmanuel Kunzmann were Hofbauer's traveling companions.

CHAPTER 4

1. *SH* XVII 248: "After two years of hermit life, he was forced to abandon it because of an edict of Joseph II."
2. XI 267, *SH* XVII 243. Emmanuel Kunzmann lived as a hermit in Tivoli for about three years (VIII 146, 147).

CHAPTER 6

1. XI 31. Johann Emanuel Veith made this claim. He relied on Father Martin Stark who knew the saint so well. Hofbauer learned of the writings of the Redemptorist' founder through Diessbach. We may assume that Diessbach also made him aware of the Redemptorist Congregation.

CHAPTER 11

1. Father Peter Blasucci (1752–1817) was superior general of the Redemptorists from 1792 until his death on May 13, 1817.
2. The church at St. Benno was not very large. When Hofbauer claims it held one thousand people, it would be only if the people were jammed inside.
3. V 120, I 85. Father Hübl preached for the first time in Polish in 1800.
4. VIII 246. The extent to which music was fostered at St. Benno is clearly shown by the inventory of musical scores present at St. Benno's suspension (IX 57-61).

CHAPTER 12

1. François-Pierre Mercier, Nicolas Lenoir, and Jacques Vannelet joined the Congregation along with Father Joseph Passerat (V 147–148).

CHAPTER 13

1. In addition to Father Vannelet, Father Passerat also wrote to Rome about this matter. Hofbauer valued Passerat a great deal. He even presented him to the General Government (in Rome) as a "model of all virtues" (XIII 321). But their characters were fundamentally different. Even their concepts of the life within the Order, of holiness and community life conflicted on many points (XIV 107). There were also accusations from Italy, from Father Isidore Leggio, who attacked the vicar general quite brutally, reproached him for not possessing the spirit of the Congregation, and for not following the prescribed rules of the Order: "You have left Italy so that you may do what you want. Is that right? You have not understood how to grasp the spirit of the Congregation. You have not grasped it. You were not here with us for even a year: Novice, professed and ordained all at once....Then you were sent across the Alps as Vicar General....I ask you to make sure that your novices at least are taught to live according to our Rule and that nothing is changed" (VIII 27–29). Different concepts of community life are clearly evident here (see also IV 139–140, VIII 21).

2. VIII 96–97. Cardinal Litta also helped to change the minds of the General Government. He wrote to Superior General Blasucci that Hofbauer was a "model of a member of the Order, full of zeal for the glory of God and full of love for the salvation of the people" (VIII 202–205). Generally, the papal nuncios in Warsaw were not sparing in their praise (V 106, XIII 328). "The behavior of the Fathers is praiseworthy in all things. They could hardly be better role models....They are the best and most zealous in Warsaw" (X 251–252, V 157).

CHAPTER 15

1. In order to disturb the flow of the narrative as little as possible, here in the notes, I only want to mention without giving dates or a description of the negotiations a few other attempts by Hofbauer to establish foundations. Rome: VIII 13, 254, XIV 100, 101, 113–117. Spoleto: VIII 163. Farchant/Partenkirchen: VIII 17–20, 35, 182, 187–188, II 33. Lindau: V 158. Constance: V 158. St. Pölten and Vienna: VIII 51, I 51, VIII 81, 201, 79. Reute/Tirol: VIII 188. Ellwangen/Schönenberg: VIII 176. Wurzbach/ Schwaben: VIII 188. In Saxony: VIII 188, 199. Schevatz/Tirol: VIII 184. Markzeling: VIII 184. In Switzerland (Zurich, Schaffhausen): V 24, 29, 58–60, 63. Kobylka in Galicia: III 92, II 67, VIII 230–231. Mohilow: VIII 190. Liechtenstein: XIV 179. Janow: I 87–94, XI 179, XIV 17–18. Worth special mention here are the two hospices at Lukjowka (VIII 108, 110, 269) and Radzymin (I 19, VI 66, X 40, 43), which were established in the vicinity of Warsaw.

CHAPTER 16

1. The negotiations regarding the foundation in Mitau had already begun in 1789 (VIII 167–169). The superior general approved missionary activity in Mitau in a letter dated February 27, 1795 (VIII 45), because the need for pastoral work was so great there. Hofbauer sent three confreres there immediately. The political situation made any correspondence between Warsaw and Mitau impossible. A catastrophe happened. On June 22, 1799, the bishop of Vilna released the three Redemptorists from their vows by his own authority and simply incorporated them into the diocesan clergy (I 13, II 35, V 4, VIII 43, 189–190).

2. Hofbauer's traveling companions were Adalbert Schröter, Franz Wiesi (? I 30) and the cleric Franz Kopsch. Franz Kopsch had already gone to Vienna in June 1797. The entire route of the journey is described in *MH* I 42.

3. There is proof that a house of the so-called "Institute of the Penitent Brothers" existed in Wollerau as early as 1792. Their community at the time consisted of four members. They had their accommodations "*im Hirz* [sic]." Brother Ignatius, one of the four Penitent Brothers was the "owner of the house and property." But Ignatius was the nephew of the village priest at the time, Father Josef Kümin. Thus one is left with the

question whether these Penitent Brothers had anything to do with the request for the Redemptorists to come to Wollerau. We may assume so (*MH* I 20) because in addition to their lives as penitents, these Brothers wanted to dedicate themselves to the Christian education of young people. Perhaps there were not enough suitable teachers and priests. Perhaps they urged the Switz government to call Hofbauer to Wollerau to establish a Latin school and orphanage in conjunction with the Penitent Brothers.

4. Perhaps unbearable tensions arose with the Penitent Brothers. Brother Anton Gallus Rief (V 76–78, XV 120, X 255, I 20) was the leader of the Penitent Brothers in Wollerau and was mistakenly identified as a member of the Redemptorist Congregation (I 10). On January 20, 1798, Jestershein wrote to Clement concerning Brother Gallus: "Admittedly his intentions were good but, as such people are, without proper consideration; meanwhile, what can be done, since God allows it?" (*MH* I 20). Clement himself made interesting and telling remarks regarding this Brother Gallus (V 76–78): "He needs a lot (of money) and lives quite comfortably on his travels...." Brother Gallus even spent the money meant for Mass intentions. Hofbauer wrote to Wessenberg on May 30, 1803: "I received reports regarding Brother Gallus Rief. He has separated himself from the young swindler, is presently staying not far from Regensburg, and has completely abandoned his plan to found an Order" (*MH* XV 120). Important connections are also listed in the pamphlet *400 Jahre katholische Pfarrei Wollerau [400 Years of the Catholic Parish in Wollerau]* (Wollerau: Buchdruckerei M. Theiler-Helbling, 1939), pp. 77–95.

CHAPTER 17

1. V 2, I 36, VIII 106. Father Hofer (*Clement*, p. 111) and Father Hosp (*Clement*, p. 72) speak of a meeting with Joseph Helg, the founder of the community of the Sisters of Perpetual Adoration [?]. Of course, that is a mistake. Joseph Helg had already died as the parish priest of Ricken on April 27, 1787. (Episcopal archives of St. Gallen, shelf no. 273.) Henri Vincent Ferrer Rigolet was his successor as parish priest of Ricken (1787–1798). He fled from the French troops on August 29, 1798. From 1802 until December 9, 1808, Rigolet was active in Klagenfurt. In 1820 he was auxiliary priest in Eggerstanden (Franz Stark, *900 Jahre Kirche und Pfarrei St. Mauritius Appenzell [900 Years of the Church and Parish of St. Mauritius in Appenzell]*), p. 125.

2. V 160. Hofbauer's traveling companions were Father Hübl, Father Franz Hofbauer, and the cleric Johannes Sabelli.

3. Since Wessenberg (1774–1860) played such a decisive role in Hofbauer's life, I want to add a brief portrait of him here. Ignatius, Baron von Wessenberg was very intelligent and just as energetic. He became the vicar general of the Bishop of Constance at the age of only twenty-eight. His position grew more and more influential. He was devoted to the reform of the Church. Many of his reforms appear very modern: he created a

new hymnal for the diocese; he insisted on more focus to the Sunday sermon; he stood up for active charity, for taking the laity in the Church seriously and for a reform of the clergy.

On the other hand, Wessenberg was a typical man of the Enlightenment. He even joined a secret society which had as its goal the dissemination of the ideas of the Enlightenment. He stubbornly rejected the contemplative Orders and pilgrimages. He also had little time for popular piety, such as devotions, and so on. His radical views were in accordance with the union of the church and state and led him to the demand that the German Church should separate itself from Rome. Behind his extreme position of rejecting the pope was a very justified interest in the revaluation of the office of bishop.

4. XV 119–121, X 254–255. Hofbauer also started an elementary school in Jestetten. Soon a high-ranking civil servant came and asked the Redemptorists to come to Tiengen in order to train schoolteachers there. Hofbauer responded: "As soon as I have enough members, we can look into the matter" (X 252–255, V III).

CHAPTER 18

1. Once again his traveling companion was Hübl. During the audience with the pope, the vicar general of the Redemptorists received from Pius VII the authorization to have his theology students ordained by any bishop (III 90). The clerics—Casimir Langanki, Franz Hofbauer, and Johannes Sabelli—also traveled with Hofbauer to Italy. The three men were ordained in Foligno on October 23 (VI 161, XI 199, VIII 111). They returned to Jestetten by way of the Gotthard Pass (VIII 113–114) and Lucerne where they arrived in mid November (VI 161). Hofbauer and Hübl left the three new priests at Mount Tabor and continued to Vienna (where they arrived on December 3). The winter was harsh. The two friends, exhausted and sick, arrived in Warsaw only at the end of January 1804 (VIII 130). Then Hofbauer received the alarming news from Jestetten about "the extreme emergency in which the community found itself" (XI 71). Clement was in Jestetten again on September 21, 1804 (XV 46).

2. IV 69, 74, 76, 77. Dr. Höhn especially, who was rumored to be an opponent of the priests, had to fear for his life (IV 70, 71, 73). The former director of the shrine fled to Villingen out of fear of the enraged people (IV 80, 85, 86). Even the government was concerned for the personal safety of this man: the authorities clearly emphasized unmistakably, however, that the Redemptorists were not responsible in the least for the people's unrest (IV 84, 129). Dr. Hörn, the director of the shrine, is even supposed to have been bodily attacked by the people of Triberg (IV 63, 64, 68).

CHAPTER 19

1. Hofbauer had a discussion with the prince's palace chaplain at the beginning of August (VI 2). Immediately thereafter the negotiations began (VI 1–8). As early as October, Hofbauer had the approval of the prince and the bishop. He had permission to begin the proposed foundation in a rented apartment (VI 6–8). In November Father Rector Passerat arrived in Babenhausen with his confreres and candidates (VI 164, 183).

2. VI 82, 45. The population of Babenhausen rebelled in January 1807. The pro-French Bavarian civil servants were driven from the chancery. The army moved in and put down the uprising. Montgelas and his followers immediately suspected the Redemptorists of starting the rebellion. The priests' house was thoroughly searched (VI 152, 43) and the Liguorians were declared public enemy number one.

   At the beginning of February, the King of Bavaria issued an order which meant the *coup de grâce* for the foundation. All Redemptorists had to leave his territories before the end of February. The priests were closely watched and all contact with the population was forbidden. The decree declared that the Redemptorists were to be escorted to the border by the military (VI 48, 44). The people of Babenhausen stood up for the Redemptorists as best they could. They collected twenty sacks of wheat for them. The farmers transported these twenty sacks to Bregenz. The farmers were punished by the authorities for this act of charity (V 153).

CHAPTER 21

1. At the time Redemptorists or former Redemptorists worked as pastors in two dozen parishes in the Upper Valais for a shorter or longer period:

Albinen:	1807–1808 (Hartmann); 1808–1811 (Schöllhorn); 1824 (Schulski)
Betten:	1812–1815 (Nosalewski)
Binn:	1808–1809 (Nosalewski)
Ergisch:	1811–1819 (Schulski)
Gampel:	1814-1818 (Johann Egle)
Gondo:	1815–1825 (Nosalewski)
Grächen:	1824-1828 (Schulski)
Inden:	1808–1810 (Jos. Hofbauer)
Leukerbad:	1808–1809 (Hartmann); 1816 (Brenzinger)
Leuk-Stadt:	1808–1809 (Sabelli); 1809 (Hartmann); 1810–1813 (Franz Hofbauer); 1813–1824 (Brenzinger)
Obergesteln:	1810–1811 (Anton Egle); 1811–1812 (Biedrzycki); 1812–1813 (Anton Egle); 1813–1823 (Forster)
Randa:	1818–1824 (Schulski)
Ried-Brig:	1808 (Forster)?
Ried-Mörel:	1809–1810 (Hartmann)
Saas:	1808–1811 (Schulski)

St. Niklaus:	1828–1848 (Schulski)
Törbel:	1810 (Hartmann); 1813 (Franz Hofbauer)
Turtmann:	1811 (Franz Hofbauer); 1811–1814 (Schöllhorn); 1813 (Schulski); 1824–1860 (Brenzinger)
Ulrichen:	1809–1813 (Forster)
Unterbäch:	1812 (Nosalewski)
Varen:	1813 (Franz Hofbauer)
Visp:	1807 (Langanki); 1807 (Sabelli); 1807–1808 (Franz Hofbauer); 1808–1811 (Biedrzycki); 1811–1812 (Baumgartner); 1812–1816 (Franz); 1815–1819 (Franz Hofbauer)
Visperterminen:	1813 (Franz); 1813 (Johann Egle); 1814–1816 (Schöllhorn)
Zeneggen:	1808 (Schulski); 1808–1813 (Johann Egle)

CHAPTER 23

1. In addition to Father Clement Hofbauer, Brother Matthias Widhalm was the only Austrian. Like Clement Hofbauer and Martin Stark, he had also moved from Küstrin to Vienna.

CHAPTER 27

1. In one convent, for example, the choir sisters were allowed to take Communion twice a week, the lay sisters only once. Hofbauer energetically fought for the abolition of this inequality (XI 122).

CHAPTER 28

1. It concerns the rules of the Order which the vicar general modified to suit the requirements in Austria. E. Hosp: *Geschichte der Redemptoristenregel in Österreich [History of the Redemptorist Rule in Austria]* (Vienna, 1939), p. 236.

CHAPTER 29

1. The following belonged to Hofbauer's inner circle of friends: the respected lecturers Dr. Madlener and Dr. Veith, the philosopher Anton Günther, the future Cardinal Rauscher, the lawyers Franz Springer and Friedrich von Held, who would later play an important role in the history of the Redemptorist Congregation. Also Pajalich, Horny, and so on. Clement Hofbauer also stood in friendly contact with professors of the Catholic Faculty of Vienna: the biblical commentator Roman Zängerle, the future reform bishop of Graz-Seckau (1824–1848); the biblical commentator Petrus Ackermann, canon of Klosterneuburg; the theologian Gregorius Thomas Ziegler, the reforming Bishop of Tarnow (1822–1827), and Linz (1827–1852); the church historian and Court Chaplain Vinzenz Darnaut. Hofbauer's influence upon these men was an important contribution to church reform far beyond Austria's borders.

CHAPTER 30

1. The Silesian poet Josef Eichendorff was a friend of Clemens Brentano. He studied law in Vienna from 1810–1813. He had contact with Clement Hofbauer through the Romantic Circle (XI 325, 329). Clemens Brentano lived in Vienna beginning in July 1813. He met Hofbauer there. The poet was not yet ready for conversion to a truly Catholic way of life. Later he remained a true friend of the Redemptorists. Hofbauer also wanted to help the poet financially at the time (XIII 54–55, XI 328).

2. It would be extremely informative for the understanding of Hofbauer and the Catholic Restoration in Austria if one traced the threads that connect Hofbauer to Diessbach and Penkler and those that connect Hofbauer with the Viennese Romantic Movement. It is interesting to note in this regard that the most influential personalities of the Hofbauer circle were almost all converts and even converted families (Schlegel, Pilat, Müller, Schlosser, Klinkowström).

CHAPTER 32

1. In 1812–1813 Vicar General Hofbauer called the two priests Johannes Sabelli and Josef Forthuber from Switzerland to Vienna for the planned educational institute [(XI 319, XII 60. Sabelli and Forthuber)]. Since the Müller institute failed, Father Sabelli remained as Hofbauer's secretary. Father Forthuber was sent as superior to Walachia (in the Ottoman Empire) when the missionary station in Bucharest was founded.

2. XI 25. The copy of the *Constitutiones et Regulae* (1782) that Father Srna was using is in the General Archives of the C.Ss.R. in Rome. In over fourteen small pages in the appendix, Srna describes his stay in Hofbauer's house in Vienna. The quotation above is on p. 11.

3. Hofbauer sent four confreres to Bucharest: Father Jos. Forthuber as superior together with Brother Matthias Widhalm and the two clerics Libotzky and Hätscher. Their situation there was quite miserable. The departure of his confreres was not easy for Hofbauer. Dorothea Schlegel wrote to her sons that the separation from his confreres had made Hofbauer very sad (XIII 276). Later the situation of his confreres in Walachia made him so depressed that he wrote to them that he wanted to cry tears of blood because he had sent them there (XV 27–28).

4. Josef Libotzky began his novitiate on September 14, 1814. The vicar general received his vows on September 27, 1815 (the only vows of a confrere that Hofbauer ever received in Vienna). Franz Hätscher received the habit of the Order on October 15, 1814, in Vienna. On December 5, 1815, he took his vows in Bucharest. The third candidate was Josef Srna. Hofbauer took him into his rooms in 1814 where he remained until he went to Valsainte (Switzerland) in 1818, where he began his novitiate.

5. The Ursulines asked that their highly valued spiritual director not be removed (XIII 133, 136). Baron Penkler, Baron Stifft, the personal physi-

cian of the emperor (XIII 136, XII 202), and others tried to intercede for Hofbauer.

CHAPTER 35

1. The Franciscans had provided them with the third floor of their house. Since the Franciscans were not very numerous, the building was almost empty.
2. XII 229. The church which had served the French troops as a stable after their invasion was consecrated on December 24 (XIII 287–289, XIV 137). Father Joseph Passerat was promoted from superior to vicar general. He arrived in Vienna on October 20 and immediately took over the direction of the novitiate (XIII 260, XIV 137).
3. Among the twenty-seven candidates there were five priest novices, nine clerical novices, three novice brothers and ten candidates for the brotherhood.

CHAPTER 37

1. XI 269, 262. We know of Hofbauer's discussion with the Protestant bookseller Friedrich Perthes. To him, Clement allegedly made the strange statement that the schism within the Catholic Church at the time of the Reformation occurred "because the Germans had and have the need to be pious. The Reformation spread and sustained itself not through heretics and philosophers but rather through people who really wanted a religion for the heart. I told this to the Pope and the Cardinals in Rome but they did not believe me. They cling to the belief that it was animosity toward religion that caused the Reformation" (Clemens Theodor Perthes, *Friedrich Perthes*, 6th ed. (Hamburg and Gotha 1872), T. II, 124–125. *MH* XI 325–328, 242).
2. Hofbauer's internal attitude, the choice of his allies and friends, and his criticism of the Roman curia must be understood on the one hand as the expression of his religious way of thinking (*sentire cum Ecclesia*). On the other hand, they must also be seen against the historical background of the times. Cf. Hofbauer's attitude to the nuncios (XI 270).
3. XI 205, 240, XII 54, 55. He complains repeatedly that no one in Rome knows enough about the German character. One hardly even makes an effort in Rome to treat the Germans properly (XIV 116–118).

   Clement wrote to Abbot Forster, who had influence in Rome, that he should forcefully present the entire distress of the German Church because "one never gets anything done with the Italians without being coarse with them....Why must the center (of the Catholic Church) be in a corrupt country? Whose entire wisdom rests in clever cunning?...I repeat: the danger in Germany is greater than the Romans want to believe" (XIV 121–123). When Severoli, the Nuncio in Vienna, writes to Cardinal Litta, it is as if one were reading a letter from Hofbauer: "It is certain that we must pay more attention to an understanding of Germany. We must learn to speak the language more fluently. We must learn to appreciate its literature and also the customs of one of the most interesting nations in all of Europe" (XIV 117).

4. XII 251–260. Particularly in his evaluation of Sailer, the candidate for bishop, Hofbauer is unmercifully harsh. We must characterize his judgment in many essential points as simply wrong (XV 13–17, XII 269). For his part, Sailer, although a very peace-loving man, responded in kind and spoke of the "godlessness and injustice of Hofbauer's pack of lies" (cf. Hubert Schiel, *Sailer*, Vol. I 605 and Vol. II 760). But that does not justify Hofbauer's judgment of and attitude toward Sailer.

We are dealing here with two typical representatives of Reform Catholicism of the time, although Hofbauer went more in the direction of a restoration. (The word restoration did not have the negative sense at the time which we attribute to it today.)

Index